Fortress • 64

The Castles of Edward I in Wales 1277–1307

Christopher Gravett · Illustrated by Adam Hook

Series editors Marcus Cowper and Nikolai Bogdanovic

First published in 2007 by Osprey Publishing

Midland House, West Way, Botley, Oxford OX2 0PH, UK

443 Park Avenue South, New York, NY 10016, USA

E-mail: info@ospreypublishing.com

ISBN 978 1 84603 027 7

Typeset in Monotype Gill Sans and ITC Stone Serif
Design by Ken Vail Graphic Design, Cambridge, UK
Cartography by The Map Studio, Romsey, UK
Index by David Worthington
Originated by United Graphic Pte Ltd, Singapore
Printed in China through Bookbuilders

07 08 09 10 11   10 9 8 7 6 5 4 3 2 1

A CIP catalogue record for this book is available from the British Library.

FOR A CATALOGUE OF ALL BOOKS PUBLISHED BY OSPREY MILITARY AND AVIATION
PLEASE CONTACT:

Osprey Direct, c/o Random House Distribution Center, 400 Hahn Road,
Westminster, MD 21157
Email: info@ospreydirect.com

Osprey Direct UK, P.O. Box 140, Wellingborough, Northants, NN8 2FA, UK
E-mail: info@ospreydirect.co.uk

www.ospreypublishing.com

Dedication

For Jane and Joanna.

Acknowledgements

The author like to thank Christine Kenyon of the Photographic Library at CADW for her help and advice, and Peter Humphries, also of CADW, for comments concerning Flint.

Artist's note

Readers may care to note that the original paintings from which the colour plates in this book were prepared are available for private sale. All reproduction copyright whatsoever is retained by the Publishers. All enquiries should be addressed to:

Scorpio Gallery,
PO Box 475,
Hailsham,
East Sussex
BN27 2SL,
UK

The Publishers regret that they can enter into no correspondence upon this matter.

The Fortress Study Group (FSG)

The object of the FSG is to advance the education of the public in the study of all aspects of fortifications and their armaments, especially works constructed to mount or resist artillery. The FSG holds an annual conference in September over a long weekend with visits and evening lectures, an annual tour abroad lasting about eight days, and an annual Members' Day.
The FSG journal *FORT* is published annually, and its newsletter *Casemate* is published three times a year. Membership is international. For further details, please contact:

The Secretary, c/o 6 Lanark Place, London W9 1BS, UK
Website: www.fsgfort.com

FRONT COVER Conwy castle. (CADW)

Contents

Introduction

The castles built by Edward I in Wales rank amongst the finest military structures in Europe. As the English king determined to stamp his authority on the province that refused to yield quietly, he directed the building of enormous structures that were as much a statement of power as they were defences.

Wales had been a target for English kings even before the Norman Conquest of 1066. Welsh princes interfered in the politics of Anglo-Saxon England, while English rulers and lords took their opportunities to invade, skirmish across the marches, or even settle along the coasts. After the conquest of 1066 the Normans settled in both north and south Wales and built their castles. English settlements were consolidated until Wales was considered a principality owing fealty to England. This, of course, was carried out without actually asking the Welsh how they felt, so it was not surprising that they wanted a say in the matter. In the north of the country was the principality of Gwynedd, with its natural stronghold of Snowdonia; further south and east was the principality of Powys. Between them lay an area bounded by the River Conwy on the west and the Dee estuary to the east, variously referred to as 'The Four Cantrefs' (as it was composed of four districts) or 'The Middle Country'. Welsh princes had fought over it, but from Chester had come English forces, ensuring that the Welsh and English won and lost the area for centuries. Welsh castles existed as well as English ones, but for permanent control the king would need to add further strongholds in this area. Edward I (1272–1307) was just the man to attempt this. A determined policy was set in motion to crush resistance once and for all.

Wales was a difficult place for campaigning, as English armies had discovered. The central part was mountainous and unsuited to cavalry and to heavily armoured troops. During the 13th century Llywelyn the Great and his grandson, Llywelyn ap Gruffydd, caused a great deal of trouble to Edward. Whilst prince, Edward had lost his lands in north Wales, since the Welsh had allied themselves with his father's enemy, Simon de Montfort. Adding insult to injury, Edward had been captured with his father after the battle of Lewes in 1265. When he returned to England as king in 1274 it was obvious that Llywelyn was spoiling for trouble, refusing to attend the coronation and plotting to marry de Montfort's daughter, who ended up being captured when the English seized her ship in the Bristol Channel.

Edward declared war in November 1276 and summoned the host to meet at Worcester on 24 June 1277. However, he had already organized his forces for war. The castle of St Briavell in the Forest of Dean was a major maker of bolts for crossbows; ships were drawn from the Cinq Ports and other areas. Edward designated three military captains to organize defence and raise militias, and to take charge of troops sent to them: in Chester and Lancaster a companion of the king, William Beauchamp, Earl of Warwick; Roger Mortimer in the shires of Shrewsbury, Stafford and Hereford; and Pain de Chaworth, who held a captaincy in west Wales, this being then taken over by the Earl of Lancaster in April 1277. They could also negotiate with local Welsh lords in order to enlist native soldiers into the ranks. By spring 1277 their bold methods had taken back everything Llywelyn had seized in the Marches from the borders of Cheshire to Cardigan Bay. Humphrey de Bohun, Earl of Hereford, recaptured his lands in Brecon, while the Earl of Lincoln took Dolforwyn and recaptured Builth. Two sons of Gruffydd ap Madog came to terms with Edward for north Powys, opening the way north and south of the River Dee. In the valley of the Tywi, Rhys ap Maredudd submitted to Pain de Chaworth and so Dryslwyn castle was available to the king. Carreg Cennen, Llandovery and Dinefwr were captured in June, the latter becoming an administrative centre. The new commander, Edmund, Earl of Lancaster, could now move north and by the end of July had seized Aberystwyth. Edward pushed Llywelyn and his influence out of east and south Wales and back to Gwynedd.

The king's successes allowed him to begin a castle-building programme at Builth, Aberystwyth, Flint, Rhuddlan, Ruthin and possibly Hawarden.

Other castles were strengthened in Wales and the Marches with small expenditure, such as Cardigan, Carmarthen, and Montgomery. Some existing fortresses were replaced, e.g. Rhuddlan replaced Dyserth, the latter built by Henry III.

A political settlement gave Llywelyn's younger brother, Dafydd, extensive areas of land between the Conwy and Clwyd rivers; he was also allowed to repair Hope (Caergwrle) castle and make his headquarters at Denbigh. However, in 1282 Dafydd launched an attack on Hawarden castle, once again provoking a Welsh revolt. Edward's reaction was swift and sharp. Writs were sent out across England and also to Ireland, Ponthieu and Gascony, for supplies and men to gather at Chester; the sheriffs of 28 shires were to muster 1,010 diggers and 345 carpenters there by the end of May, less than two months after the revolt began. Three armies marched into Wales: in the north from Chester, in the centre from Shrewsbury northwards and from Montgomery westwards, and in the south from Carmarthen north-eastwards. Whatever Edward may have intended by his actions, the killing of Llywelyn that same year in an ambush near Builth allowed the king to put himself forward as the feudal heir to the forfeited land. The Welsh princedom was replaced by a royal English master. Denbigh was seized after a siege lasting for a month in the autumn, while Dafydd was captured in June 1283 and subsequently hanged, drawn and quartered. The king set about organzing the building or rebuilding of such lordship castles as Denbigh, Hawarden, Holt and Chirk, to guard his rear, and could now march into the centre of Gwynedd. The castles of the Welsh princes – such as Castell y Bere, Criccieth and Dolwyddelan – were seized, and the royal fortress ring expanded in 1283 when work began on major new castles at Conwy, Harlech and Caernarfon. Edward now had the great engineer Master James of St George in his employ, and these new castles showed a strength of purpose that is less evident in those of the first campaign. In August and September the Cinq Ports fleet was instrumental in placing forces in Anglesey and Edward ordered a bridge of boats to connect to the mainland near Bangor, so that a central army under Otto de Grandson could land near Caernarfon and then proceed to Criccieth and Harlech. Luke de Tany crossed in November only to be ambushed, with 16 knights and their squires drowned. The bridge was eventually finished, and was later deliberately destroyed once work was under way at Caernarfon and Harlech.

A plan view of Aberystwyth castle. Begun in 1277, it was of lozenge shape, and had a single inner gatehouse. It appears originally to have been of part-concentric plan, with only a single line of wall on the south-west side. However, after 1282 this side too was given an inner wall, achieved by building a circular (then D-shaped) tower along the southern wall of the inner curtain, with presumably another on the other side, the two joined by a new stretch of curtain to form a fourth inner side. The stretches of old curtain left in the newly formed outer ward were demolished. A mural tower was also added midway along the new curtain, overlaying a lime kiln, presumably used in the original construction works of 1277 onwards. The alterations were probably the work of Master James of St George after the capture of the castle following its partial demolition in 1282. (Adam Hook)

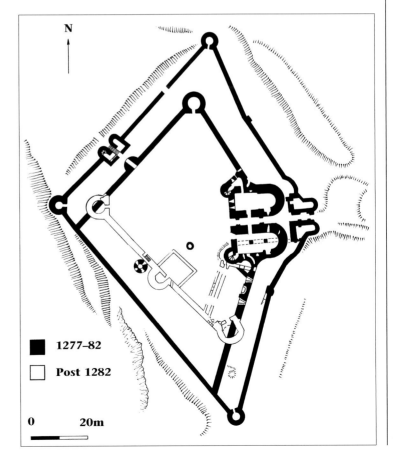

N

■ 1277–82
□ Post 1282

0   20m

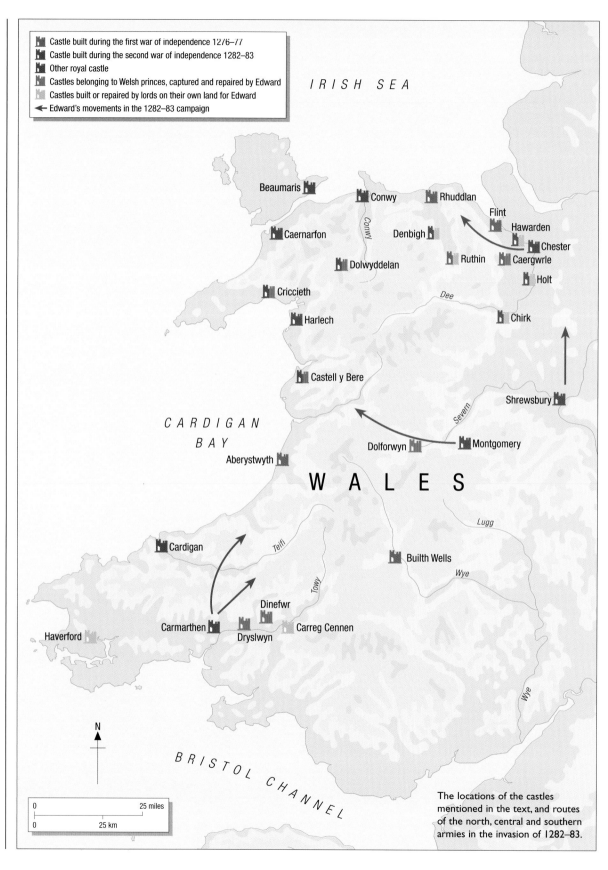

Castle built during the first war of independence 1276-77
Castle built during the second war of independence 1282-83
Other royal castle
Castles belonging to Welsh princes, captured and repaired by Edward
Castles built or repaired by lords on their own land for Edward
Edward's movements in the 1282-83 campaign

IRISH SEA

Beaumaris

Conwy

Rhuddlan

Flint

Hawarden

Caernarfon

Denbigh

Chester

Ruthin

Caergwrle

Dolwyddelan

Holt

Criccieth

Chirk

Harlech

Castell y Bere

Shrewsbury

CARDIGAN BAY

Dolforwyn

Montgomery

Aberystwyth

WALES

Lugg

Cardigan

Builth Wells

Wye

Dinefwr

Haverford

Carmarthen

Carreg Cennen

Dryslwyn

Wye

N

BRISTOL CHANNEL

0   25 miles

0   25 km

The locations of the castles mentioned in the text, and routes of the north, central and southern armies in the invasion of 1282-83.

The concentration on castle building in north Wales reflected the need to confront the Welsh rebels concentrated in Gwynedd and Snowdonia. Most were built along the north or west coast, allowing supplies to be brought by sea. Rhuddlan was further inland but a canal altered the course of the River Clwyd to achieve the same end. Castles within reach of the borders could receive supplies from England.

A lesser revolt occurred in 1287, and in 1294 a third war broke out. Gascony had been confiscated by Philip IV of France and Edward asked parliament for funds to raise an army to fight in France. The Welsh and Scottish objected to this and, in Wales, Madog ap Llywelyn rebelled, resulting in several sieges and several castles still under construction being overrun, including Denbigh. Despite severe damage being inflicted on the unfinished castle at Caernarfon, the English replied by repairing the castle so thoroughly that it became a fortification of immense power. Notwithstanding, in 1295 Edward ordered work to begin on yet another castle, this time at the eastern end of the Menai Strait, at Beaumaris in Anglesey. In October 1295 the Scots made an alliance with France, and Edward was forced to declare war on both, switching his focus to them. Here his interference stirred up the revolt of William Wallace, and Scottish unrest continued after the latter's execution in 1304, now largely in the shape of Robert the Bruce. Edward had his hands full with this Celtic problem until his own death in 1307.

Edward's five castles of Flint, Rhuddlan, Conwy, Harlech and Beaumaris were new structures placed to assert lordship in a time when many castles were developments of existing structures. Even Caernarfon, built over a Norman site, was essentially a new build. Edward found additional support in the new castles erected by English marcher lords: Hawarden, Denbigh, Holt and Chirk. Many other existing fortresses were improved and strengthened both in Wales and on the borders. New towns were a feature of Aberystwyth, Flint, Rhuddlan, Caernarfon, Conwy and the seigneurial castle of Denbigh.

It was at Caernarfon that Edward's son and namesake was born in 1284 and here presented to the people as the first English Prince of Wales. The title has been continued ever since for the eldest son of the monarch. According to David Powel in the 16th century, Edward announced at Rhuddlan that he would appoint a prince born in Wales who could speak no English, which turned out to be his own young son.

The castle at Aberystwyth, set near the sea, was huge but is now ruinous. The tallest surviving tower (shown here) is from the inner ward. (CADW)

Chronology

1255	Llywelyn ap Gruffydd emerges as the leader of Gwynedd and re-establishes its power. He imprisons his brother, Owain, probably at Dolbadarn.
1267	Treaty of Montgomery: Henry III acknowledges Llywelyn ap Gruffydd as Prince of Wales.
1272	Death of Henry III. Accession of Edward I.
1276	Llywelyn refuses homage to Edward I.
1277	First Welsh War against Llywelyn ap Gruffydd. Gwynedd taken by Edward. Treaty of Aberconwy sees Owain released. Edward builds or repairs castles at Flint, Rhuddlan, Ruthin, Hope (Caergwrle), Builth, Aberstwyth, and possibly Hawarden. Dolforwyn castle besieged and surrenders to the English; refortified.
1278	Dolforwyn granted to Roger Mortimer.
1282	Second Welsh War with Llywelyn ap Gruffydd.

	Death of Llywelyn. Aberystwyth castle and town badly burned.
1283	End of Second Welsh War. Work begins on castles at Conwy, Harlech and Caernarfon.
18 January	Dolwyddelan castle captured from Welsh and then refortified.
14 March	Criccieth castle by now captured from Welsh; it is refortified and given a free English borough.
25 April	Castell y Bere captured from the Welsh, refortified and a town built.
June	Dafydd captured and executed.
1284	Work begins about this time on castles at Denbigh, Hawarden, Holt and Chirk. Prince Edward (future Edward II) born at Caernarfon. Statute of Rhuddlan creates new counties of Anglesey, Caernarfon, Merioneth, Cardigan and Carmarthen, with Caernarfon as the centre.
1287	Revolt of Rhys ap Maredudd.

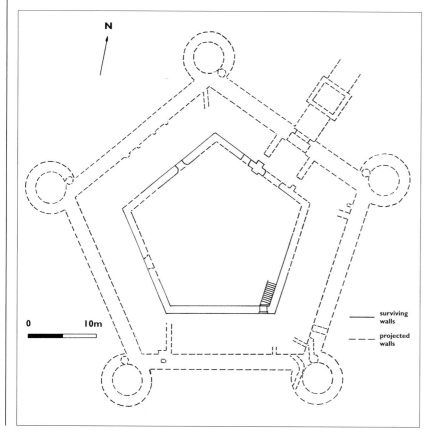

N

0   10m

surviving walls
projected walls

LEFT The castle of Holt, overlooking the River Dee, was known in the Middle Ages as Chastillion or Castrum Leonis (Castle of the Lion). It was a lordship castle built between 1282 and 1311 by John de Warenne but there is little known of its building history. It is now much destroyed but appears from archaeological, written and pictorial evidence to have been a regular pentagon with cylindrical angle towers, with the ground then scaped to it. Unusually the square chequer tower before the gate stood on a rocky pinnacle about 30ft square (see the barbican at Warenne's castle at Sandal for a parallel). The castle probably derives from Aberystwyth and Rhuddlan; the widely spaced gate towers are paralleled at Conwy. (Adam Hook)

RIGHT The great hall and service area provide the west range of the inner ward at Harlech. From left to right: the kitchen; the entry passage; the buttery and pantry; and the hall, which would have had a wooden screen across to shield the main room from draughts from the doorway (roughly on a line with the notice board).

1292	Rhys captured and hanged.
1293–94	Third Welsh War, against Madog ap Llywelyn.
1294	Caernarfon overrun by Welsh rebels; Castell y Bere besieged and disappears from the records. Denbigh and other castles under construction overrun.
1295	Work begins on Beaumaris castle and resumes at Caernarfon.
1297	Edward invades Scotland.
1298	Work on Beaumaris all but stops.
1301	Prince Edward created Prince of Wales. Work on Caernarfon ceases.
1304	Work resumes on Caernarfon.
1306	Work resumes on Beaumaris.
1307	Death of Edward I. Accession of Edward II.
1327	Death of Edward II. Accession of Edward III.
1330	Work ceases on Beaumaris.
1377	Death of Edward III. Accession of Richard II.
1399	Richard II stays at Conwy, then Flint, where he is captured and taken to London. Abdication and murder of Richard. Accession of Henry IV.
1400	Owain Glyn Dŵr declared Prince of Wales and goes into revolt. Rhuddlan town damaged but castle holds out.
1401	Conwy captured by the Welsh.
1403	Caernarfon besieged by Owain. Beaumaris besieged.
1404	Harlech and Aberystwyth captured by Welsh troops after long sieges. Caernarfon besieged again. Criccieth falls.
1405	Welsh routed and Beaumaris recaptured by the English.
1408	Harlech besieged by the English.
1409	Harlech captured by Henry of Monmouth (future Henry V).
1413	Death of Henry IV. Accession of Henry V.
1422	Death of Henry V. Accession of Henry VI.
1461	Harlech held by Lancastrians in Wars of the Roses.
1468	Harlech surrenders to Yorkists under Lord William Herbert and his brother.
1642	First Civil War breaks out.
1644	Montgomery captured by Parliamentary forces.
1646	Beaumaris, Conwy, Caernarfon and Rhuddlan surrendered to Parliamentary forces. Harlech besieged.
1647	Harlech surrenders to Parliamentary forces.

Design and development

Edward I took a personal interest in his new castles. He was usually present at the inauguration of the work, where he might discuss the finer points with his master mason so that he was satisfied with the plans.

Where possible a castle was sited on bedrock to provide a solid base and to deter enemy mining. If not possible, timber piles might be driven; if the ground was soft a timber raft might be constructed.

The Cistercian abbey of St Mary lay on the site of Conwy town, and was rebuilt elsewhere. It and the Hall of Llywelyn not only offered stone but accommodation for men of rank during construction, as happened also at Rhuddlan (Blackfriars) and Beaumaris (Greyfriars). Also, being the burial place of Llywelyn the Great, placing a castle and town there had obvious significance.

Construction

Costs of construction in Wales were enormous and not assisted by rising prices. Edward lavished £27,000 on Caernarfon, a huge amount spent not only on the castle but also the walls and towers of the fortified town that rose with it; indeed, the cost continued into the reign of his grandson, Edward III, and the castle was not completed even then. Conwy also had a town wall, costing £14,000, built from 1283 to 1287. Three other castles bore similar expenditure on town as well as castle walls. £14,400 was spent on Beaumaris, which again continued into the reign of Edward III and was never finished, so this figure in no way represents a total cost. The powerful fortress at Harlech is a more modest £9,500. From 1277 to 1282 the castle, town walls, bridge and dyke at Rhuddlan cost £9,613 2s 8¼d, of which £6,940 17s 5d went on wages. Between 1277 and 1282 the sum of £1,666 9s 5¼d was spent on Builth castle but the Barons of the Exchequer were keen to see an audit, since it was £167 10s 6¼d less than the revenue sent there. Edward, in his desire to subdue the Welsh, spent about £80,000 on his Welsh castles, almost double the costs involved in rebuilding Westminster Abbey. By comparison, in 1290 his best tax year yielded £116,000 and other years much less.

A king instructs his master mason – a depiction of the building of Clifford's Tower from the early 14th-century *Lives of the Offas*, by Matthew Paris. Master James and his colleagues would have appeared very much like this. The right-hand illustration shows craftsmen with plumb line and set square (By permission of the British Library, Ms Cotton Nero 1D, f.23v.)

Despite their size and cost, Edward's castles rose with commendable speed. Flint took eight and a half years (1277–86); Harlech took seven and a half years (1283–90); Builth took five and a half (1277–82); Conwy took five years (1283–87); Rhuddlan took four and a half (1277–82); and Caernarfon (1283–c.1330) and Beaumaris (1295–c.1330) took longer, though by February 1296 Beaumaris had inner curtain walls at least 6.1m (20ft) high and in some places 8.4m (28ft). It is also worth bearing in mind that several castles were under construction or being rebuilt at once: from 1277 Aberystwyth, Builth, Flint and Rhuddlan; from 1283 Harlech, Conwy and Caernarfon; and from 1295 Beaumaris.

On 29 February 1296, Master James wrote to the king's Exchequer from Aberconwy, regarding the cost of work at Beaumaris:

In case you should wonder where so much money could go in a week, we would have you know that we have needed – and shall continue to need – 400 masons, both cutters and layers, together with 2,000 less skilled workmen, 100 carts, 60 wagons and 30 boats bringing stone and sea coal; 200 quarrymen; 30 smiths; and carpenters for putting in the joists and floor boards and other necessary jobs. All this takes no account of the garrison mentioned above, nor of purchases of material, of which there will have to be a great quantity … The men's pay has been and still is very much in arrears, and we are having the greatest difficulty in keeping them because they simply have nothing to live on. (McNeill, 1992)

We are fortunate in that not only the Pipe Roll accounts survive for such work but also the originals of the enrolled copies of manuscripts that came into or out of the Exchequer, as well as the royal Chancery and the household. The numbers employed in construction are impressive: in 1295 some 3,500 men were at work at Beaumaris during the summer, while Harlech employed about 1,000 men per week in the summer of 1286. Several castles might be under construction or renovation at the same time and so bodies of workmen might move from one to another. In order to draw on this massive labour force Edward enforced his right to military service rather than the Anglo-Saxon and Norman burh and castle work. Special commissioners were appointed to hire craftsmen. Contracts were only used for small areas of the work. Now, however, wages were paid to the masons, who were employed on a daily basis or else received an agreed amount for an agreed job, this being called task-work. It became the norm in the 14th century for castle work, as well as for civil building projects. The Crown also developed powers to impress the necessary men, which was only popular with the monarch. The costs account for nearly two-thirds of the money spent on these projects.

Workmen were drawn from all over England; the fenlands resulted in Lincolnshire contributing 150 ditch diggers (similarly Yorkshire) in 1282–83, while Norfolk and Suffolk provided 100, as did Northamptonshire and Cheshire; by contrast Cumberland only sent ten. Woodcutters came predominantly from the West Midlands, these counties providing around 1,600 of them to clear the routes. The main assembly place for the workforce was Chester, from where the men moved into north Wales, but in May–June 1282 a total of 30 masons sent from Gloucester, Somerset and Dorset went to Bristol and thence by ship to Carmarthen, from where they moved overland north to Aberystwyth. One account in 1277 notes that workmen from Yorkshire destined for the building works at Flint and Rhuddlan should have had an escort of three mounted sergeants each paid 7½d per day – not for their protection, but to stop them from running away. Despite this, there is not much evidence of problems with this

The great hall at Harlech with its fireplace visible between windows that looked out towards the sea. To the right, along the north side, is the chapel, whose west wall retains traces of plaster. In both rooms the line of beam holes were for the ceiling whilst the corbels held a penthouse roof, marked also by the stringcourse. The bakehouse was to the right of the chapel.

large workforce, but it did mean there was a shortage of labour to be employed by other lords; indeed, so much was spent in Wales, not only on materials but on wages, that by the time Edward moved up to Scotland men found their pay falling into arrears, and went on strike.

The most important persons were the master masons, with Master James of St George at the top of the tree. He was from Savoy and had been brought to Britain by Edward, who had spotted him during his travels. Master James brought his style of design with him and in 1278 was sent to Wales. He was paid two shillings per day, a week's wages for other craftsmen, rising to three shillings for life in 1284, plus a manor in north-east Wales. By the following year Edward had created him 'Master of the King's Works in Wales' and in 1290 Master James was made constable of Harlech castle – a rarity for a mason. When the monarch moved up to Scotland the Savoyard went with him, though he kept his manor. He died in 1309, his castles a lasting monument to one of the greatest architects of medieval England.

Savoyard influences have been identified by A.J.Taylor not so much in the layouts of the castles as in several architectural features: the spiral (helicoidal) form of putlog holes for scaffolding, semicircular arches (the outer gate at Harlech being similar to Saillon); inverted semi-conical latrines set on corbels from wall faces (e.g. the outer curtain at Harlech, as at La Bâtiaz, Valais, Switzerland); triple finials on the merlons (Conwy and perhaps Harlech); and the shape of the windows at the back of the gatehouse at Harlech, which are very like a design at Chillon in Switzerland. The king was influenced by these styles during his travels, but Master James was not alone in using them; other craftsmen and administrators were involved.

A corbelled latrine turret on the outer south wall at Harlech. This is reminiscent of Savoyard work at La Bâtiaz in Switzerland. (CADW)

The master mason undertook a dual role in the building project, as he was also the main architect responsible for the planning of the building, in conjunction with the king. Walter of Winchester acted as clerk of works to Master James at Beaumaris, a post that had arisen during the century. One master working with Master James of St George at Conwy in 1286 was John Francis, probably another Savoyard (builder of Saillon and probably Brignon in 1261–62), together with Jules of Chalons, William of Seyssel and Peter of Boulogne. English masters included the master engineer Richard of Chester, who in 1283 was sent to Chester to gather tools for rock cutting and to recruit masons and stone-cutters. In the 1286 account are found Roger of Cockersand (Lancashire), John of Sherwood (Nottinghamshire) and Robert of Frankby (Wirral). Walter of Hereford carried out much of the work at Caernarfon once Master James had designed it, which may explain the lack of Savoyard touches. Giles of St George and Adam Boynard may have held key positions as masons under Master James in the earlier stages of the Harlech works. Master Bertram, probably from Gascony, was an *ingeniator* (military engineer) but also worked on the castles at Dolforwyn, Rhuddlan and Bere, as well as at Caernarfon in 1283–84. Master Manasser de Vaucouleurs came from Champagne. Under Master James he worked on the well at Hope (Caergwrle), payment being calculated at 6d per toise (the normal unit of measurement for masonry surfaces in the castle works of the counts of Savoy). He received costs for 7 toises or approximately 60ft. He was also master and director of the diggers at Caernarfon.

The work was not always of high standard. In 1280 the new justiciar of West Wales, Bogo de Knovill, reported that Aberystwyth castle gatehouse had its foundations too near the ditch and was jarred by the sea. The town gates were

permanently open and had no locks nor bars; moreover, he found no garrison, arms, nor provisions and no workforce at the quarry for the town walls. In 1282 Master George was to be found there, ordering what appear to be radical re-designs as well as repairs following the Welsh revolt.

Freemasons finished ashlar blocks and also decorated capitals, corbels, traceried windows etc. in the main rooms of the castle. Below them came the rough masons who cut the blocks to the required shape ready for laying by the layers. Hewers or quarriers used hammers and rods to prise stone slabs free from the quarry walls. Mason's marks can be found on some stones but these may have been added at the quarry, rather than at the building site. Large quantities of mortar were required and this was made by lime-burners, who burned limestone from Anglesey to produce quicklime. A. J. Taylor calculated, from the accounts for Flint from April 1279 to August 1281, that about 87,000 bags of lime were provided. Two sieves are mentioned at Hope castle for mixing the mortar. Water provided the easiest method of transport and boatmen were needed to supply their craft for loading. Carters also carried stone and wood to the workforce at the building site. Some sites may have had a treadmill crane, rather like a giant hamster wheel powered by men to wind the rope on the crane. A windlass is mentioned in the 1319 account for Caernarfon and may have been used to lift stones.

If a suitable quarry was near at hand, it was utilized. At Rhuddlan dark purple sandstone was used for the lower courses of towers and curtains, while yellow sandstone was used for the upper areas of towers. Light red sandstone was used for window frames, and also embrasures in the inner ward. A grey limestone was used mainly for the curtains and wholly for the revetment of the moat; it was also used in places mingled with the yellow sandstone. At Conwy much of the dark Silurian grit probably came from a quarry near the Llangelynin road, being used for both castle and town walls. Yellow-brown rhyolite for areas of town wall and

Flint castle was one of the first to be built by Edward I, with work starting in July 1277. Now ruinous, the ground and first floors of the donjon (right) remain.

OPPOSITE **Construction**
Building castles required vast resources and manpower. Here the Savoyard style of helicoidal scaffolding has been erected, the horizontal supporting beams thrust into putlog holes that spiral up the newly constructed walls. At Harlech the north curtain wall has a row of eight putlog holes sloping up from left to right for scaffolding used in the 1280s, while the south curtain has two rows for two such ramps. Similarly at Beaumaris, the inside of the western curtain has three lines of sloping scaffold holes, which also appear in other areas.

Set squares and plumbs were used to ensure correct angles and levels. As well as a master mason and his deputy there were bankers (cementarii), layers (cubitores) and dressers (batrarii); the Caernarfon record for 1316–17 shows the latter work was actually done by the layers. There were mortar makers, mortar carriers (fauconarii), sand throwers, water carriers, hodmen (hottarii), barrow men (portatores ciuerum), carpenters, watchmen to control the workmen, and carters. The diggers (fossatores) at Builth in 1278 included 36 women, each receiving 6d – one penny less than the male diggers.

The interior of the donjon at Flint, showing the openings in the basement wall and the wedge-shaped rooms on the floor above. The room at right centre (with a gap in the outer wall) once housed the winch mechanism for the drawbridge. The spiral stair was at the far right, and latrine shafts are present in the cross-walls. The well shaft is just visible on the upper floor at extreme left. (CADW)

spur wall were also found locally. A pink sandstone was the freestone used in finishing windows, loops, door jambs etc., from the Creuddyn peninsula across the river. Beaumaris was largely built of limestone, sandstone and metamorphic schist, all found locally. This meant that finely carved decoration was kept to a minimum because of a lack of easily available freestone, being confined mainly to the chapel vault and arcade; the stone brought by sea was guarded by a fleet between Anglesey and Snowdon. At Flint the unfinished walls of the towers were protected by 44 bundles of thatch during the winter months of 1281–82.

Carpenters provided the huge amounts of timber necessary even in a stone castle: scaffolding poles (2,000 at Conwy in 1286), beams and planking, floorboards, joists and ceiling beams, turning bridges, doors and drawbars, window shutters, partition screens, lean-tos and wooden buildings in the bailey, animal pen fencing, even toilet seats. Initially carpenters might well be required to provide palisade fencing to protect the workforce in enemy territory. Philip 'Senta' was principal carpenter working on the donjon roof of Flint in 1286, probably the same Philip ('of Ewyas') working at Caernarfon in 1295 and the 'Philip the Carpenter' there in 1305. Largely in charge at Conwy in 1286 were the carpentry masters Henry of Oxford and Laurence of Canterbury. Timber came by boat from Trefriw and further afield.

The inner side of the triple-towered gatehouse at Denbigh, with the Great Kitchen Tower on the right.

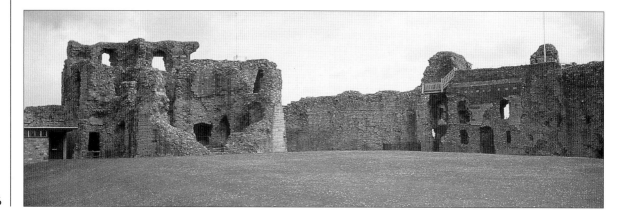

Smiths were needed to sharpen tools as they were blunted with continual use, or worse, broke. They had to provide huge quantities of nails (125,000 for Conwy in 1286) as well as window bars, door and shutter hinges, latches and bolts. Iron, steel and nails, bought in quantity at Newcastle-under-Lyme, came across to Chester before transferring to ships. Flint supplied coal for furnaces for the smiths, and lead for roofs etc., shipped across over the Irish Sea. Lead also came from Snowdonia and the Isle of Man. Plumbers had to insert the lead piping and cistern linings, and add lead to roofs; in 1286 lead being cast at a foundry near Ewloe for the roof of the donjon at Flint was guarded constantly. Bundles of brushwood were needed for plumbers (in 1284 twelve cart-loads at Flint). Simon the Glazier from Chester brought glass for Caernarfon in 1283 and probably also provided it for Conwy. Slate was used for roofing and also occasionally for bedding and levelling courses, perhaps coming from Llangelynin either by boat or overland. Carriage for all the materials was immense: in 1286, for transporting to Conwy (for work on the castle and town walls) 524 tons of sea-coal, 140 carrats of lead, 90 summe of iron, 3 barrels of steel, 500 lb. of tin, over 106 tons of sand and sundry other items, the total cost was £105 3s 5¾d.

The castles at Criccieth and Conwy retain traces of plastering that show they were originally designed to stand out white against their setting. This idea of highlighting the castle is also seen in the banding of Caernarfon and the figures and pinnacles that once set off the battlements of such fortresses. All this, together with expensively painted or woven banners, was designed to point out lordship as surely as had the Norman donjon before. If any building had taken its place it was now the great gate, with its multiple defences and suites of rooms above. Stephen the Painter had worked in Savoy, and surviving work on the walls of the *camera clericorum* at Chillon suggest similarities with the decoration used in Wales.

The army of workmen were sheltered in wooden huts and firstly the ditchers (*fossatores*) were set to work to carve out the castle ditches. Building work was carried out with constant defence in mind. At castles such as Builth, Conwy and Beaumaris a barricade was erected to protect the workmen digging the moat and constructing the walls; within that at Caernarfon timber buildings with eight chambers were erected complete with glass windows, for the king and queen to hold court. At Harlech the first season, completed by the winter of 1283–84, saw the construction of the main inner curtain wall and towers of the castle to a height that would serve to protect the soldiers and work force, some 4.5m (15ft). Nor were the walls initially built to their full thickness but only about two-thirds, this being finished latterly in 1289 either by thickening internally or externally. At Beaumaris work began in 1296 and within a year the inner curtain stood. At Caernarfon in May 1305 a horn was purchased at 7d presumably to sound the beginning and end of the working day.

The remains of the gatehouse at Denbigh castle, with its striking chequered masonry. Begun in 1295 for Henry de Lacy, the statue above the passage may represent Edward I. The castle was set in the south-west corner of the town walls built some 13 years earlier.

The great tower at Flint, begun c.1281 and finished in 1286, was basically a cylindrical keep that was a development of the earlier square or rectangular donjons of the 10th–12th centuries and which was already rather out of date. Here, however, the internal design is unique. Instead of having a number of wooden floors carried on beams perhaps above a vaulted basement, the thickness of the walls at the base – 7m (23ft) – carries a barrel-vaulted passage which opens at intervals into the central basement where the walls are dressed ashlar. Above is rough stone but no evidence for a vault; presumably it was at least covered in timber. Within the passage is a well that could also be reached from the floor above via a hole in the vault. Above basement level the external walls are much thinner, because the inner section forms a platform for five separate rooms; possibly the inner wall here was polygonal rather than cylindrical. One room formed a chapel, with a stone piscina. Three had a latrine, three an embrasure. The centre may have been left open to the light. There was at least one and possibly two floors above this one. Prince Edward of Caernarfon came to Flint in 1301 and it was probably for this visit that a wooden structure was erected on the top and the stone matched to it, while lead was brought for the roof.

A. J. Taylor's work on the building accounts for Beaumaris reveals the following defence measures in the first building season (18 April–29 September 1295):

Naval patrol: wages for Sir Henry de Lathom and 95 sailors keeping the sea between Snaidon and Anglesye together with 20 crossbowmen = £151 2s 6d.

The garrison: wages of William de Felton, esquire-at-arms, constable of the aforesaid castle, and of 22 fellow guards dwelling with him, with their horses and arms, in the garrison of the aforementioned castle, 1 May to Michaelmas, 152 days at 12d a day each = £129 0s 8d.

The steps down to the sally-port at Denbigh allowed access to the foot of the mantlet wall on the west side of the castle, in front of the town walls.

Wages of Adam de Haskayt, esquire-at-arms, and of 100 foot archers dwelling with him in the garrison of the aforesaid castle, 12d a day for himself, 4d a day for each of 5 twentymen, and 2d a day for each of 95 archers = £194 5s.

Wages of Simon de Cremplesham and his 19 fellow crossbowmen staying together in the aforesaid garrison, 6d a day for himself and 4d each for his 19 fellows = £52 12s 4d.

Wages of Master William the artiller and his servant, staying in the garrison aforesaid for making and reparing crossbows, quarrells and other necessaries, 9d a day for himself and his servant = £5 15s 6d.

Wages of Master Richard the engineer and Master Thomas the engineer, esquires-at-arms, repairing engines as required, 1 May–10 July, 71 days inclusive, the one taking 12d, the other 9d a day = £6 4s 3d.

Total = £387 17s 9d.

From 29 September 1296 onwards, the archers disappear from the garrison lists, leaving the 20 crossbowmen.

Flint

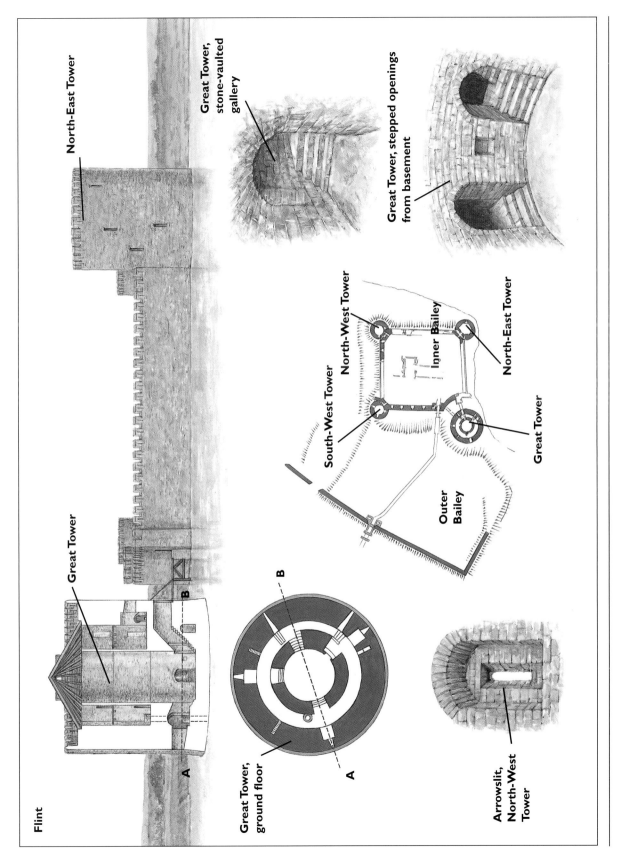

North-East Tower

Great Tower

A

B

Great Tower, stone-vaulted gallery

Great Tower, stepped openings from basement

North-West Tower

South-West Tower

Inner Bailey

North-East Tower

Great Tower

Outer Bailey

Great Tower, ground floor

B

A

Arrowslit, North-West Tower

Design

Edward's castles in Wales display several designs. The old motte and bailey castle at Builth Wells, destroyed by the Welsh in 1260, was rebuilt by Edward in 1277 with a 'great tower' or donjon, harking back to an earlier style. Flint, also begun at this time, consists of an inner and outer ward, the former nearly square in plan with cylindrical corner towers; however, the south-east tower, separated by a ditch, is much larger and is in effect a donjon (it is called the 'great tower' in a contemporary document). The castle has no gatehouse, just an opening in the curtain near the donjon, which guards the approach as well as the river and both wards. A similar layout is seen in certain contemporary French castles such as Dourdan and Yverdon and more especially at Aigues-Mortes, with its large Tour de Constance built by Louis IX. It may be relevant that Edward had embarked from this town in 1270 on his way to the Crusades. However, apart from its positioning the actual details of the Tour de Constance are dissimilar to those of the donjon at Flint, whose internal arrangements (the basement has a broad mural passage around a central room) are seen nowhere else. The donjon was obviously also designed as an impressive domestic suite (possibly for the king's son, Edward, in 1301), since it was provided with some sort of wooden viewing gallery around the summit. The cylindrical donjon on the old motte at Hawarden, probably of the 1280s, has an octagonal upper interior.

A form of donjon is perhaps seen again at Caernarfon in the Eagle Tower, the most massive of the towers set at the western end of the single enceinte. It was at one stage occupied by Otto de Grandson, who became Justiciar of North Wales, rather than the king himself. Grandson had come from Savoy, from where ideas of castle design, as demonstrated by James of St George, had eminated.

Criccieth castle from the north-east is seen here perched on its outcrop of rock, with the gatehouse prominent.

Moreover, he was close to the king; one story recalled how he had sucked poison from a wound in Prince Edward's arm made by an assassin's knife while in Syria. Both Caernarfon (1283–1330) and Conwy (1283–87) were built essentially as fortified enceintes fitted to rocky bases, but this does them little justice. The strong curtain walls at Caernarfon are pierced by passages; the mural towers, polygonal at Caernarfon and cylindrical at Conwy, are immense. Both castles were divided into two wards by a cross wall, providing a more private inner sanctum for the king. Conwy does not have a major gatehouse, but the eastern and western entrances are guarded by the proximity of the neighbouring cylindrical mural towers, plus a barbican. Both castles were integrally connected by towered curtains to the new fortified towns that grew up with them, although at Caernarfon the latter was so close that it left little room for a defended approach. Moreover, the site was fairly level, though a wide moat separated castle and town. Conwy would have stood out on its rocky site, its limewashed walls, turreted inner ward towers and pinnacled battlements all adding to the effect of a breathtaking statement of royal power. James of St George's polygonal walls at

The inner side of the gatehouse of the inner ward at Criccieth. It is difficult from its ruinous state to determine exactly what work was carried out by Edward I following his capture of the castle but he may have heightened this gatehouse.

21

The square donjon of the Welsh castle of Dolwyddelan, built by Llywelwyn the Great c.1221–40. After its capture, Edward I may well have added a storey to it but the battlements and line of mock drains are Victorian additions. The West Tower (to the right) may also be Edward's work.

Caernarfon may have echoed Constantinople, but this was not the first time he had used the design; before his employment by Edward he had used such towers at the palace of St Georges-d'Espéranche (from whence came his own name) for Count Philip of Savoy, who was a relative of King Edward. Indeed, the latter may have visited it on the way back to England in 1273 to take the crown.

The third form of castle was the concentric defence. Rhuddlan (1277–82) has a lozenge-shaped inner curtain with opposing gatehouses at the east and west angles (their timber back extensions have now gone), and a four-storey cylindrical tower at the north and south angle, with a basement in the latter. The outer wall set with rectangular bastions is beautifully symmetrical, surrounding the inner defences except on the south-east side where it runs down to the river. Similarly Aberystwyth became a concentric castle of lozenge shape. At each corner of the diamonds, towers or gatehouses were strategically planted to defend all sides of the castle. Harlech (1283–90) is sited on a rocky outcrop above the River Dwyryd and has an irregular rectangular enceinte set with large cylindrical corner towers and a massive gatehouse. The outer curtain wall, by contrast, is very low and revetted to the rock, so that the outer ward is little more than a platform. While it follows the inner curtain closely it has no towers other than a small twin-towered eastern entrance and a twin-towered postern to the north. To the west the rock has been cut to form platforms for catapults, the whole surrounded by a wall running from the north-east angle to enclose the rock before sweeping back along the western side to include the 'Gate next the Sea'. Beaumaris was the last of Edward's castles, begun in 1295 but never finished; building had stopped by 1298 and began again in 1306, though work more or less ceased in 1330. It has an almost square enceinte with cylindrical towers at the angles and a D-shaped tower in the middle of the western and eastern sides, while great gatehouses (similar to that at Harlech) occupy the middle of the northern and southern sides, the latter complete with a barbican. The outer ward was protected by a fairly regular curtain set with cylindrical towers liberally supplied with loops, with a gate to the north and a 'Gate next the Sea' to the south with a spur wall overlooking a dock, near the proposed town wall. Beaumaris has been described as the most perfect concentric castle, although the gatehouses of the outer ward are offset from their counterparts on the inner, to prevent an enemy rushing straight through both. Nevertheless, had it been completed it would have been one of Edward's most abiding works.

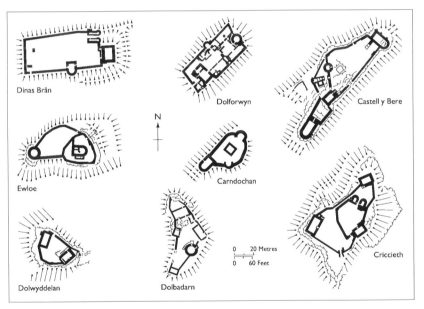

Dinas Brân

Dolforwyn

Castell y Bere

N

Ewloe

Carndochan

0   20 Metres
0   60 Feet

Criccieth

Dolwyddelan

Dolbadarn

Castles built by Welsh princes are often irregular in plan to fit the terrain and tend to ignore flanking towers. At Ewloe and Carndochan D-shaped towers acted as donjons; at Dinas Brân and Dolforwyn similar towers were set along the walls. All were eventually captured by Edward's troops but only some were partially rebuilt. Dolforwyn fell in 1278 and was given to Roger Mortimer. Dolwyddelan and Castell y Bere fell in 1283 and were reworked. Dolbadarn became a royal manor.

Lordship castles

The king was not alone in building or repairing castles in Wales. Baronial fortifications were erected in splendid fashion by powerful marcher lords. In the north-east borders the king would create a new lordship and usually agree the design with the lord of the place before helping with some of the huge costs involved. Lords met costs from funds raised from taxes and rents levied from farmers in areas under a lord's control, together with revenues from sale of goods and livestock and finally from his own private income. Henry de Lacy, a commander in the first Welsh expedition, was granted the lordship of Denbigh in 1282 together with the captured castle. Although never fully rebuilt it has a strong enceinte set with towers. A triple-towered gate faces the new borough; these towers, together with the mural towers on this northern side, are polygonal and the masonry banded, echoing the positioning of Criccieth and

Near the top of the curtain wall at Conwy can be seen the row of 12 latrines; grooves for the wooden fronts and seats are still visible on some of them, and they voided into the mill leat or else the Gyffin stream. A wooden hall probably stood near here, completed in 1283 for the King's wardrobe and connecting with the timbered back of the Mill Gate; the upper floor of the latter was probably occupied by the controller of the wardrobe. Nearby there also seems to have been the office of the 'master of the king's works in Wales'. The large staffs of these departments could well be the reason for the multiple privies. For other known contemporary multiple sanitary arrangements one has to look to some of the monastic houses. (CADW)

the symbolism of Caernarfon. Edward assisted de Lacy by paying £22 for the transport of timber, provision of fencing and workmen's new tools. Hawarden, given to Roger de Clifford, has a circular tower on an earlier motte. Now largely gone, Holt (John de Warenne) was once a single enceinte of regular pentagonal design, with mural flanking towers. Chirk (Roger Mortimer) also benefited initially from royal assistance. Ruthin (Reginald de Grey) had a single enceinte divided into two wards, as did Haverford (bought by Queen Eleanor).

Carreg Cennen in Carmarthenshire was seized during Edward's first campaign. John Giffard, followed by his son, rebuilt the fortress. John, or perhaps the king, strengthened the inner ward with mural towers at the north-east and north-west angles and built a sturdy gatehouse between them. From here a stepped ramp barbican (recalling Goodrich) forced an enemy to make two left turns before approaching the gate itself. The more vulnerable western and southern sides of the castle were given an outer wall with angle towers and gate; thus Carreg Cennen is concentric where needed, as again at Goodrich.

Edward's designs must have influenced castles elsewhere. Late 13th-century English examples of new powerful gatehouses are Goodrich (also with a barbican), Tonbridge and Rockingham. At the triangular castle of Caerlaverock in southern Scotland (whether built by Scots or English is uncertain) a powerful forward-thrusting gatehouse, balanced curtain walls, cylindrical angle towers and

Conwy castle seen across the rooftops from Tower 13, showing the extent of the contemporary town wall, probably the finest surviving in Britain.

a wide moat with an outer, effectively concentric bank, all echo the elements seen in the king's Welsh castles. Similar designs were being seen on mainland Europe, some probably influenced by Welsh examples or else already responding to the ideas coming to Wales. In the early 14th century, Clement V's castle of Villandraut in Guyenne, a balanced rectangle, had a strong gate, angle towers and moat. Others displaying influences include Muiden (Netherlands), Hanstein (Germany) and Marschlins (Switzerland).

Welsh castles

Some castles were captured by the English from the Welsh princes and then rebuilt either as royal or lordship castles. 13th-century Welsh castles are usually irregular in plan, since they were shaped to natural features. Curtain walls are low and often lack flanking towers; each tower was seen as an entity in itself and rarely exceeded two stories in height, with a roof set well below the battlements. Some towers had one side curved out where they faced the field, to form a slightly elongated 'D' shape, used also to form donjons at Carndochan (near Bala) and Ewloe (near Hawarden). Entry was often through a gateway in the curtain wall and elaborate gatehouses were rare; the one at Criccieth in Caernarfonshire may well have been modelled on Beeston in Cheshire.

At Criccieth an outer line of walls encircled a promontory on Tremadoc Bay, with an inner ward complete with twin-towered gatehouse. How much rebuilding was carried out by Edward I after its capture in 1283 has been hotly debated. Much of the outer walls is ruinous so any reconstruction has largely rested on archaeology plus documentary evidence of the costly building work. At first it was thought it was constructed by the Welsh in two phases, then that the inner ring was the work of Edward. Now it is considered that both wards were originally Welsh work but that Edward largely spent his money on heightening the gatehouse, refortifying the south-east tower in the inner ward, and extending the outer gatehouse, probably done by William of Drogheda, the mason working on Harlech on the other side of the bay. The walls of the inner ward were plastered to stand out white, as much a statement of power as at Conwy. The town itself was another of Edward's planted boroughs.

Dolwyddelan (captured 1283) probably had the west tower and keep worked on. Castell y Bere, taken the same year, also had work carried out and a town was established. In the south, Dinefwr (forfeit 1277) and Dryslwyn (captured 1287) in Carmarthenshire were also repaired.

Not all captured Welsh castles were rebuilt. Dolbadarn simply had timbers removed, since the castle's strategic importance was eclipsed by the great new royal stronghold at Caernarfon. Several English-built royal castles already existed too, namely Carmarthen, Cardigan, Montgomery, Shrewsbury and Chester.

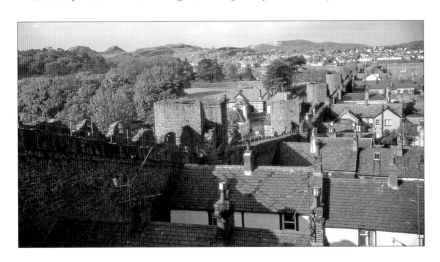

The Mount Pleasant and Town Ditch Road section of the Conwy town walls, on the south-east side of the town. The open-back design can be seen clearly.

Towns

In Wales new castles were a major influence on the rise of new towns, or 'plantation boroughs'. It has been estimated by Soulsby that about 80 per cent of towns during the medieval period owed their origins to the presence of a castle. The large numbers of people who were needed to build it and the staff who then continued to man it had the same requirements as everyone else. Food, clothing, work tools and raw materials prompted market needs and thus a borough, which could increase its wealth from burgage plots, fines and tolls. The new development might petition for a charter enabling the townsfolk to elect a mayor, hold courts and a weekly market; the houses and shops would benefit from being enclosed within walls and the king could encourage settlement by Englishmen by offering burgages at low, fixed rents. Until the arrival of the Normans significant urban development, unlike in England, had been slight; moreover, a castle offered security in what was to the newcomers a foreign land. At this early period there was often a large gap between the castle being built and a town following, as barons weighed up the pros and cons. During the 13th century this process speeded up. All of Edward's major castles were provided with a new town beside them.

Towns were often provided with walls, though Flint and Rhuddlan had earth and timber defences and Harlech, which had no fortification, was protected by the shadow of the immense castle. The walls around the town at Beaumaris were only added some years after the Welsh had seized the place in 1403 and lost it again two years later; a wall footing by the dock indicates an initial willingness in 1295 but the pleas of the townsmen to Edward never bore fruit and the point where the wall joined the 'Gate next the Sea' was made instead into a turret rising from the moat, leaving the town without even a ditch and rampart until about 1407.

It has been said that these Edwardian creations are like the bastides erected in Gascony, some of which indeed the king had had a hand in founding. However, the latter did not normally have a castle and were often of geometric design, though some new towns in Wales, like Flint and Caernarfon, had a grid plan of streets. Unlike the Welsh boroughs the bastides were not built to protect a foreign body of people.

The castle was given first priority for siting to take advantage of all natural defences, such as cliffs, hills or rivers; the town followed. Edward's boroughs received far less in money for the process. Only at Denbigh, a lordship castle, was the reverse the case and even here the castle, placed in a corner, dominates the borough. In the third season at Conwy in 1284 the town defences received approximately one-seventh of the sum allowed for the castle. The castle at Rhuddlan was set next to the town but the River Clwyd was diverted in the process, to allow access to shipping.

Conwy, with its 1,300m run of walls, had 21 open-backed D-shaped towers. The Cistercian monastery on the site (where Llywelyn ab Iorworth had been buried) had been transposed to Maenan. At Caernarfon the symbolism of the castle as a seat of imperial power is reflected in the lack of polygonal 'imperial' towers and banded masonry on the town walls. Here the town is small, with only eight towers along some 700m circumference.

Towers 6 to 9 on Town Ditch Road in Conwy. Note the change in colour of the stonework on Tower 6 in the distance.

The principles of defence

The castles of Edward I are some of the most strongly defended structures in Europe. The site for each was all important. Solid rock was a major obstacle to the pickaxe and helped prevent a mine being driven under a wall; Harlech perches on a great outcrop that also defies the use of siege engines except from the town side, where the castle was further protected by cutting a man-made ditch to compensate. Conwy too is built along a rocky site. Rivers were used to provide a natural obstacle, as were estuaries. Caernarfon castle is protected on the west by the Menai Strait and along the south side by the River Seiont. In addition, the River Cadnant flowed past the north-eastern town walls. Conwy castle and town are guarded on the east by the River Conwy, while the south side of the castle has the Gyffin stream. It meant that a ditch or moat only needed to be dug to separate castle and town. Rivers also meant that during construction there was an easy road for materials and, once built, vessels could bring up provisions. Moreover, the castle could control traffic moving on it. Beaumaris was a low-lying castle and so, perhaps influenced by the work of the Clares at Caerphilly, a large wet moat was provided. As well as looking picturesque, a moat deterred miners, since the weight of water would probably collapse any tunnel that was dug under it. Many moats were dry but often sufficiently muddy to slow an attacker. They had sheer sides that might be revetted in wood or stone to offer a still smoother surface. At Rhuddlan the sides were revetted in stone and a palisade topped the steep side of the outer bank. The area by the river was wet but the rest of the moat was dry and separated from the lower on each side by a cross wall. A dry moat might be set with stakes or scattered with caltrops to slow an advance and make better targets for archers. The moat at Flint filled with water at high tide.

Curtain walls were high and thick; on average the inner wall at Rhuddlan is 9ft (2.7m) thick, whilst that at Beaumaris is 4.7m (15½ft) thick, sometimes with a battered plinth to thicken the base of the wall against miners, and sometimes buttressed. The walls of Caernarfon and Beaumaris castles are pierced respectively at main- and first-floor level by passages with flat-shouldered vaults, to provide communication between adjacent mural towers and to access latrines set in the wall thickness next to the towers. At Criccieth steps in the inner ward lead to one of two latrines cut into the curtain's thickness, whose chutes discharged on to

Beaumaris castle in Anglesey was the last castle to be built by Edward in Wales, begun in 1295. It is a classical concentric design complete with wet moat. (By kind permission of Anthony de Reuck)

Tower 9, the adjacent curtain and the 'Gate next the Sea' beyond at Beaumaris. They all display light limestone on their lower courses but darker limestone above. (By kind permission of Anthony de Reuck)

the outer wall face, as did those of latrines on the wall-walk above (now lost). The mural passages at Caernarfon are also provided with embrasures, which, with the wall-walk, allow for three tiers of fire. The lower, outer walls and towers at Beaumaris are pierced by no less than 164 loops but when the battlements were present with their own pierced merlons it is estimated that some 300 loops could be used. Here, too, each centre face of the inner curtain was provided with a box machicolation jutting out on corbels to overlook the base of the wall. The merlons on the wall heads were often provided with an arrow loop and those at Conwy, and probably also Harlech, were each topped by three simple finials for an eye-catching finish. The town wall at Conwy displays multiple corbelling to help carry a wider wall-walk; the overhang thus created also had the advantage of stopping rainwater running down the wall face beneath. The entire circuit of the inner walls of Beaumaris had the wall-walk carried on a stone corbel table.

At battlement level the merlons are frequently provided with arrow loops; these were often set at different deliniations to provide differing fields of fire. Those at Conwy are set at regular alternate levels to assist in covering the ground in front from various angles. Conwy also has creasings at the base of the parapets and towers round the wall-walks, showing that lead flashing has been removed and that the tops of the walls were (at least from this evidence probably of c.1346) covered with lead. Sometimes wooden shutters were hung between the merlons, with the slots for the pivots visible at Caernarfon. Also at Caernarfon several loops were each served by three archers via separate embrasures feeding to the loops themselves; it allowed three archers to keep up a withering hail of arrows that came out of one slit but commanded a wide radius. Alternatively some embrasures were provided with three outlets. Wooden hoardings were shed-like structures built out from the walls and provided with slots in the floor to allow defenders to command the base of the wall. Several castles show the tell-tale rows of holes to carry the beams supporting these structures; the necessary timbers might be stored in nearby towers. At Conwy they are set one beneath each arrow loop both along the wall and on the towers. Machicolated battlements carried out over the wall face on corbels were expensive and tended to be confined to gates and towers. Originally the curtain walls of Rhuddlan and Harlech had *échaugettes*, or lookout posts (*garrita*) built at the centre of the wall-walks. The four faces of the inner curtain each had a box machicolation added near the midway point to increase cover to the area of wall furthest from the angle towers. The walls were pierced with loopholes, with rebates for shutters on the inner walls and towers.

The sections of wall were usually provided with mural towers. For the most part these towers were either D-shaped, with the curved side facing the field, or else cylindrical. This meant there were no angles or corners to offer a target for a miner's pick, nor blind spots on the battlements caused by corners where crenels were lacking. They sometimes display a battered appearance, that is, they almost imperceptibly narrow as they rise, so that their bases are thicker, the better to withstand attack by mine, ram or catapult. The towers were provided with loops that allowed archers to enfilade the neighbouring section of curtain wall. Each tower could usually be closed off by doors, effectively sealing a section of wall if an enemy gained possession. However, to assist rapid movement by the garrison, some castle towers were provided with a mural passage running round through the thickness of the outer wall of a tower and joining to the wall-walk on either side. Windows (of any size) were often protected by iron grilles, their existence evident today by the fixing holes around the window openings. Tower interiors were often provided with a fireplace and could be used as accommodation.

At Rhuddlan the towers of the outer walls are square and each is provided with steps down to a barred door leading into the moat. Thus, if an enemy reached the moat, he could be met by a large body of men who had clambered down from the towers of the outer ward. However, three of these towers latterly had their openings blocked; presumably they were felt to be too much of a risk. Denbigh was provided with a complex sally-port guarded by a portcullis and door, and also a well-protected postern gate.

A few of Edward's castles are of concentric design. The best is Beaumaris, which although not completed nevertheless illustrates the fully developed design. The inner and outer walls mutually support one another, the inner following the outer closely and giving the impression of symmetry even though the sides are not actually balanced. The average gap between the walls is 18.3m (60ft). Harlech's rather low-level outer curtain is little more than a chemise clinging to the rock below the huge inner defences, a fender for the latter and providing a platform for archers, while a level area nearby was a platform for siting catapults or ballistas. However, the outer gate with its solid turrets juts out aggressively in front of the massive inner gatehouse. At Rhuddlan the outer wall follows the inner on three sides before running down from both corners of the south-west side to join the Port Gate. The inner ward is quite symmetrical, being an almost perfect diamond with gatehouses at the eastern and western corners. At Beaumaris the outer towers had three tiers of loops, while the curtains had two (battlements and ground level).

A corner tower on the low outer ward curtain at Beaumaris. (By kind permission of Anthony de Reuck)

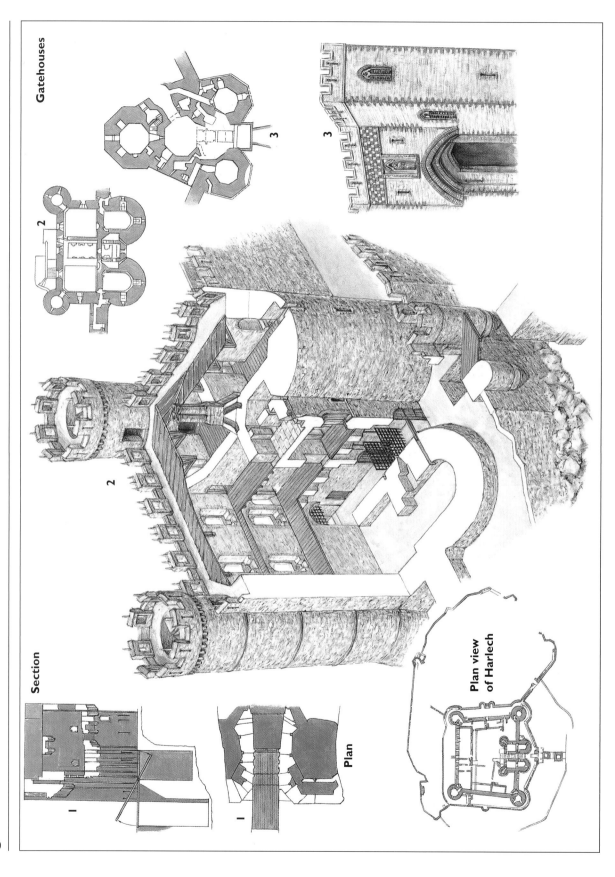

Gatehouses

Section

Plan

Plan view
of Harlech

Gatehouses

The great gatehouse is a feature of a number of Edward's castles and they are deservedly the most impressive part. They represent the peak of development in this area, turning what was a hole in the walls into the most heavily defended part of the castle, in effect an aggressive defence. In such structures the gate passage is flanked by two huge towers, usually (except for polygonal examples at Caernarfon and Denbigh) D-shaped to the field or else cylindrical. Uniquely, the Mill Gate on the town wall at Conwy has one cylindrical and one D-shaped

OPPOSITE **Gatehouses**

The King's gate at Caernarfon (**1**, shown in section and plan view) is one of the most powerful of gatehouses, begun in 1283. In front of the entrance is a turning bridge; the front end rose up into a recess while the rear dropped into a pit behind. The passage was heavily defended: if the gatehouse had been completed it would have had no less than five wooden doors and six portsculli along its length. Evidence in the existing walls suggests that the never-completed rear section made the passage turn at right-angles, thence over a second drawbridge before arriving in the lower ward.

In order to enter the great gatehouse at Harlech (**2**), the visitor was required to pass the outer gatehouse with its twin turrets and turning bridge, the pit into which it dropped forming an additional obstacle. Then followed the main gate passage, arched throughout its length and flanked by huge towers. The first obstacle was a two-leaved door closed by a drawbar running into a slot in the wall thickness. There followed two portsculli, behind which

was another door with drawbar. Further down the passage was a third portcullis, with possibly yet another set of doors in front. The room directly over the gate passage was a chapel flanked either side by a vestry but it also received the two forward portsculli when raised; the third came up into the larger of the two rear rooms. The fact that this floor housed the winches for operating the portsculli suggests it was used by the constable. Above was another floor, a residential suite laid out the same way and presumably designed for the king or some persons of rank. The rear of each tower was provided with a stair turret and, additionally, a door on the first floor at the rear led on to a platform and thence to an external stair to ground level, allowing access when all the gates were shut.

Master James of St George probably designed the splendid triple-towered gatehouse at Denbigh (**3**); once past the twin towers at the front, a vaulted hall was entered (with a chamber on the floor above). The rear tower blocked further egress, forcing a right turn into the ward.

31

tower. The flanking towers on gatehouses tend to run backwards into the courtyard, to allow extra room for domestic accommodation on the upper floors, with stair turrets at the rear corners. Some originally had timber constructions built against their rear. They are provided with arrow-loops; in the case of the King's Gate at Caernarfon some of these are multiple examples, as seen on the nearby wall heads. They are pierced by access passages to facilitate movement around the walls. The gate passage itself is always guarded by an array of defences. The vaulted passage roof is pierced by so-called 'murder holes' to allow unpleasant objects such as arrows, bolts, stones, boiling water or hot sand or pitch to be poured on the heads of attackers below or, perhaps more likely, cold water to put out any fires that might be started. Some passages are supplied with a series of pointed arches that would have to be floored over for the room above but gaps or slots were presumably left to overlook the passage below. If the gate at Caernarfon had been completed it would have had no less than five wooden doors and six portsculli along its length. The latter were iron-shod wooden grilles (occasionally all metal) dropped via grooves cut in the sides of the passage; they could either reinforce a door or cut off a group of attackers who had penetrated the passage, and could be dropped quickly to block the way in an emergency. At ground-floor level, doors from the passage led into side rooms. These might be divided into a porters' room (perhaps with fireplace) leading to a guardroom with arrow-loops facing into the passage. Town walls also had rather elaborate gates; three at Conwy each had two flanking towers.

Both at Harlech and Beaumaris (the North Gatehouse on the inner wall) an external stair links the courtyard and first-floor rooms, a handy insertion when all the gates of the passage were closed. At the latter, the towers of this gate are the only ones to approach the probable 60ft (18.2m) intended for the finished castle. The two gatehouses at Rhuddlan, rising through four stories, are set at the angles as at Caerphilly.

The triple-towered gatehouse at Denbigh has loops opening into the vaulted hall from the adjoining tower rooms and passages through the wall thickness that provided access to the curtain wall-walks from the upper stories. It also had a seated statue over the gate, of Edward I himself perhaps, in which case it may be a nod to a generous sponsor from Henry de Lacy.

Caernarfon, Harlech, Rhuddlan, Beaumaris and Aberystwyth all had impressive gatehouses, yet not all Edward's fortress work shows such constructions. At Conwy the gateway is protected by two mural towers; by raising them on the line of the rocky outcrop they are slightly further apart than was usual but the entrance is still heavily defended, with deep arrow loops from the towers allowing archers to enfilade the wall and gateway. The gate was protected by a row of machicolated battlements to command the wall directly below. There was a drawbar each side of the entry, then a portcullis with, behind, a two-leaved wooden door with drawbars. A flight of steps up on the right led from the wall-walk to the portcullis winch chamber over the arch. Behind were the upper floors with two guard rooms (now gone) either side of the passage. The gate also has a barbican set before it, forcing anyone entering the castle to make a sharp left turn after negotiating a drawbridge in front of the barbican and climbing up towards the door. The barbican wall is set with low open turrets that use the rock to form a steep obstacle externally. Access from the outer to the inner ward was similarly protected by a drawbridge over a pit, leading into a small gatehouse, while the private exit from the inner ward was of similar design to the main gate, relying on the corner towers and another, larger, barbican. Beaumaris also had a barbican set within the outer ward to guard the main South Gatehouse looking toward the dock. It was begun after 1306 because the outer walls had only reached about 8ft (2.4m) in height, and has a round rear-arch in Savoyard style. Unlike that at Conwy it had no turrets; a shooting platform allowed archers to spray the interior space.

Like Conwy, the castles at Flint, Holt and Chirk lack gatehouses, though it is possible that the gatehouse at Chirk was destroyed in the 17th century.

At Criccieth the gatehouse of the inner ward is set as far as possible from that of the outer, necessitating a long approach under the noses of archers on the high inner wall. The twin-towered gatehouse is now thought to be the work of Llywelyn ab Iorwerth of c.1230, probably heightened later by Edward I.

The turning bridge

By this date many castles were equipped with turning bridges rather than the earlier drawbridge that pivoted at the rear and was winched up via chains through slots in the wall. The turning bridge pivoted somewhere midway along its length,

Defensive features

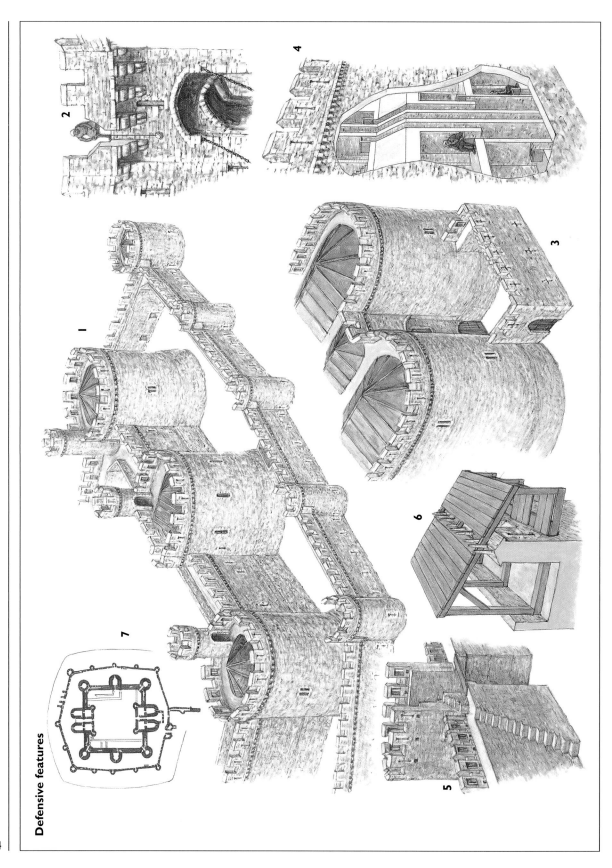

creating a see-saw effect. The rear end was weighted with stone or metal weights and held in the 'open' position by bolts or else chains from its rear edge to a winch house in a room above. When released, the rear portion pivoted down into a stone-lined pit, whilst the front portion was quickly swung up to the vertical, often into a recess in the wall face. This was a much swifter method of lifting the bridge than winching. Lifting the vertical rear end to lower the bridge once more was carried out by winch but the important thing was the increased speed in closing off the access when necessary, the pit being an additional obstacle to an attacker. For some reason the turning bridge guarding the approach from the town to the outer ward at Rhuddlan was apparently abandoned soon after completion, since the chases for the counterweights were blocked. The approach over the moat was usually via a wooden bridge on supports, often a framework with or without bracing. When the moat was dug at the new castle of Flint in 1277, a stone causeway connecting town to castle was left proud of the rest. Timber soleplates were laid on this submerged causeway and trestles inserted into them to carry the bridge. This was probably seen as a temporary structure for the new castle to function in a potentially hostile land. In about 1286, however, a stone gatehouse was constructed complete with a turning bridge, so the original bridge was taken down. The new one was supported on vertical timbers that rested on masonry piers below water level. The turning bridge itself was fitted with weights beneath the rear end, these being accommodated in rebates in the base of the front wall of the gatehouse when the bridge was raised.

The inner side of the South Gatehouse at Beaumaris. The walls may never have risen much beyond their present height.

OPPOSITE **Defensive features**
(1) The concentric defences at Beaumaris: the inner wall dominates the outer and allows twice the firepower. The mural towers have battered plinths to thicken their bases against undermining and allow missiles dropped to bounce out at unpredictable angles. The wet moat deters mineshafts. (2) A cutaway view of the machicolations over a gate at Beaumaris, showing how they might be used. (3) A simple barbican defending the South Gatehouse at Beaumaris. (4) The inner curtain at Beaumaris is served by numerous latrines in the wall thickness, with vents rising to the wall heads. The staggered-level arrow loops in the battlements can also be seen above. (5) Interior view of one of the D-shaped towers in the outer walls at Conwy. (6) Wooden hoarding used to command the base of a wall at Conwy. (7) A plan view of Beaumaris.

A tour of a castle: Caernarfon

The great castle at Caernarfon sits at the junction of the Menai Strait and the little River Seiont. The latter passes on the castle's south side and the Strait on the west, while a great ditch protects the north walls. In design the castle is a long oval enclosure running approximately east–west, whose powerful walls are set with equally powerful towers. The shape is slightly waisted in the middle, where further fortifications divide the interior into an upper ward (east) and lower ward (west). Aspects that mark out Caernarfon castle from other Edwardian castles may be linked to one event. In 1283 bones were dug up at Caernarfon that were ascribed to Magnus Maximus, the father of Emperor Constantine, the first Christian ruler of Rome. All the castle towers are polygonal rather than cylindrical, in all probability a deliberate nod to the 5th-century Theodosian walls of Constantinople, as was the different-coloured stone course running along the wall faces. Although the walls the castle copied were not built by Constantine this was unlikely to have been known at the time. Edward may well have been suggesting to the Welsh people that he was to be likened to a Roman emperor, or that this castle, unlike his others with their cylindrical towers, was to be the residence of the official ruling Wales, be it a lieutenant or a royal prince yet to be born. When Prince Edward was born at Caernarfon in 1284 it was no coincidence.

Beginning on the west side and moving south, the Eagle Tower, with more imperial connotations, begins the run of building completed during the period 1283–92. It is the most westerly of the mural towers and the largest in the castle,

Caernarfon castle, begun in June 1283, seen from the south across the River Seiont. The Eagle Tower is on the left and the town wall runs off to the extreme left. The polygonal shape and coloured banding based on the walls of ancient Constantinople can be seen.

with more mural chambers and three turrets. It was probably originally built as a lodging for Sir Otto de Grandson, a royal lieutenant and also Justiciar of North Wales. Steps on the waterside lead up to an entrance into the basement for those arriving by boat, guarded by a portcullis and double doors. Stairs from this passage in walls about 18ft thick would have led to the Water Gate on the town wall, which was built next to the Eagle Tower but left unfinished. A further passage had been intended to connect with the basement of the domestic range abutting the north wall. Opposite is a second door leading up into the Outer Ward, from where a similar door led into the ground floor. Here on the left was a stair connecting to the upper floors and to the right a small octagonal chamber presumably used as a chapel. Passages led to portcullis chambers for the postern and the Water Gate door. The first floor was the main room of the tower, with larger windows and a trefoiled piscina in the octagonal room, indicating that it was definitely a chapel. One mural room is traditionally said to be the birthplace of the first Prince of Wales, but it is more likely that the main chamber would have been the venue, if this floor had been built by then. There is evidence in the main room that a pitched roof had originally been intended here, but after 1300 a second floor (one mural room here possibly a kitchen), ramparts and turrets were added. Remains of stone figures, including helmeted heads and an eagle, remain on some battlements.

From the Eagle Tower the curtain wall runs south-east, the first part of the section of walls and towers largely built between 1283 and 1292. The wall here has a second, lower walk, probably intended to be covered like that further east. Foundations of a building set against this wall remain. The Queen's Tower is the first of the line of mural towers on the south side. It has three stories connected by a spiral stair in the north-west corner, while a mural chamber in the north-east was a chapel on the upper floor and probably also in similar chambers on the lower floors. Wall passages connected to the wall-walks. A single large turret rises from battlement level, with a small hexagonal chamber on the way to the top. This tower was known as the Banner Tower in the 14th century and a hole in a lintel above the steps would have housed the base of a flag staff.

The massive Eagle Tower at Caernarfon, which is in effect a donjon. Complete with three turrets – more than any other of the mural towers – it may well have been the residence of Otto de Grandson. The two doorways would have led into the Water Gate but the latter was never constructed. Only the beginnings of the arch and the portcullis slot are to be seen.

PAGES 38–39 **Caernarfon**

Caernarfon castle is one of the grandest anywhere and deliberately makes a statement about Edward's lordship in a hostile land. The polygonal towers and banded masonry recall the walls of Emperor Theodosius' triple defences at Constantinople. The single circuit of walls effectively divides the castle into a lower ward and more private upper ward. The Eagle Tower begins the run of building work dated to 1283–92. Effectively a sort of donjon or a tower house, it was probably originally built for Sir Otto de Grandson, a royal lieutenant and also Justiciar of North Wales. Visitors by boat ascended steps on the waterside to an entrance into the basement. Passages led to portcullis chambers for the postern and the Water Gate door. Beyond the Eagle Tower the wall has a second, lower walk, probably covered in; there remain foundations of a building set against this wall. The Queen's Tower is next, with the Chamberlain Tower beyond. Between them stood a great hall, with buttery and pantry at the east end, where now steps lead down to a postern gate. The curtain wall thickness is here pierced by two additional wall-walks complete with loopholes. The Upper and Lower wards were divided by walls running from the Chamberlain

Tower to the King's Gate. In the upper ward additional wall-walks run to the Black Tower, partly built on the old Norman motte, which forces a kink in the line. Midway along the curtain juts the Cistern Tower with a stone-lined cistern tank. The Queen's Gate is built at a height because of the motte and was provided with a flight of stone stairs to a turning bridge. Next comes the small Watch Tower with pentise roof. The eastern town wall joins the castle at the North-East Tower, whose turret has arrow loops below the battlements. The next section of curtain is the later, northern, run built mainly between 1296 and 1323, which does not include wall passages nor banding on the stones. The Granary Tower has a well serving the inner ward. The curtain either side is supplied with multiple arrow loops like those on the upper floors of the King's Gate. The King's Gate was originally intended to be the main entrance, with a drawbridge, six portsculli and five sets of doors, but was never completed. Moving westwards, a kitchen range abutted the curtain wall between the gate and the Well Tower; a section of curtain joins with the Eagle Tower and completes the circuit. The town wall circuit runs from the Eagle Tower to the North-West Tower.

37

Caernarfon

Key

1	Eagle Tower
2	Queen's Tower
3	Chamberlain's Tower
4	Black Tower
5	Cistern Tower
6	Queen's Gate
7	Watch Tower
8	North-East Tower
9	East Gate
10	Granary Tower
11	King's Gate
12	Well Tower
13	Great Hall
14	Lower Ward
15	Upper Ward
16	Multiple arrow loops.
17	Wall passages and embrasures (three-tier firing system)
18	Pivoting wooden shutter on Watch Tower
19	Kitchen complex (next to Well Tower)

Beyond lies the Chamberlain Tower. Along the curtain wall connecting these towers lie the foundations of a great hall some 30.5m (100ft) long. The remaining moulded plinth at the west end testifies to the lost glory of this building. At the opposite (east) end would have stood the buttery and pantry, where now steps lead down to a postern gate. A door in this corner gives access to the Chamberlain Tower. The curtain wall itself contains two additional wall-walks within the thickness, set with loopholes.

The Chamberlain Tower (Treasury Tower or Record Tower) is of three stories. Again, a chapel is housed in the north-east corner on the first floor. Wall passages run round the outer side at first- and second-floor level, connecting with the curtain wall passages and wall-walks. The turret has the only chimney to survive in the castle; the turret battlements are restored. The Chamberlain Tower stood opposite the King's Gate, and foundations running across between the two mark the boundary between the lower and upper wards. In the upper ward the Black Tower is reached by further wall-walks (the first-floor walk now without its roof). There is a kink in the curtain where it crosses the line of the Norman ditch around the old motte.

The Black Tower is reached from the curtain wall passage, being built partly on the side of the motte; therefore there is no ground-floor entrance and only two floors, both of ten sides internally. The upper had a chapel and ante-chapel in the thickness of the wall. Unlike other towers, steps led across the roof and it may be that it was proposed that an additional floor would be added, when the stairs would be replaced by a mural passage. The lower passage then runs to the Queen's Gate but the upper passage comes to a dead end. Midway along this section of curtain the Cistern Tower juts out from its front face. Like the Black Tower it is entered from the curtain wall passage into a small, six-sided, vaulted room. Above is the stone-lined cistern tank, open to the sky for collecting rainwater, with a stone outlet discharging from a shaft in the Queen's Gate. The cistern is seen from the wall-walk reached via stairs from the middle wall passage, which is unroofed. The top of the tower seems unfinished but would have reached the same height as that of the Queen's Gate.

The Queen's Gate is the most easterly sector of the castle, with a passage defended by polygonal twin towers. The locality of the motte meant the gate was built at a height and consequently a stone stair climbed up to the doorway, protected by a turning bridge (the pit remains), murder holes and loops. A porter's lodge was provided in the ground floor of each tower but because the gate was unfinished the northern tower is lacking its back wall, while two of the murder holes can be studied in section, as can a wall passage over the gate intended to connect to the curtain wall passages either side. A hall was to have been built over the entire upper area of the gatehouse.

The curtain wall now runs north-west, passing the small Watch Tower that juts from its outer face. Originally this was also reached from the wall-walk into its upper part, with pentise roof. In this area the battlements retain grooves for wooden shutters. The North-East Tower is the next in the curtain, an octagonal tower with a turret unusually provided with arrow loops below the battlements. The eastern town wall reaches the castle at this tower. The curtain wall passages continue through the outer wall of the

The Granary Tower at Caernarfon castle, with the King's Gate and Well Tower beyond. The two mural towers are each of four floors. The arrow loops above one another on the curtain wall at extreme left each serve two openings behind, so that one soldier in a passage within the curtain and another in a passage or embrasure in the Granary Tower can shoot through the same loop.

The rear of the King's Gate at Caernarfon. The toothings for adding stonework to the vertical wall ends suggest it was never completed. The gate passage opens into what would have been a right-angled turn with portcullis groove visible on the corner to the right of the small doorway. Above the gate passage was a chapel, and on the floor above a hall, marked by the large windows. The two blocks of three embrasures at the centre of this wall are multiple arrow loops, each block feeding one loop. At far left can be seen ground-level embrasures serving single arrow loops.

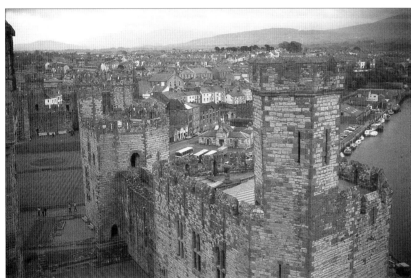

The Queen's Tower with its prominent stair turret, looking towards the Upper Ward. Beyond is the Chamberlain Tower, the concreted area denoting the lost wall separating the two wards. The well can be seen in the grass.

North-East Tower but stop at the junction with the next section of curtain, for this is the end of the earlier build and the beginning of the construction largely dating from 1296–1323, which does not include such passages. Beyond this tower the dark banding on the stones also stops. The wall now runs westerly as it approaches the King's Gate. The Granary Tower is the last of the mural towers and, like the Well Tower, is octagonal, with four stories and a turret. It also has a well reached by a mural passage on the ground floor. The curtain either side is set with multiple arrow loops, similar to those on the upper floors of the King's Gate, which the wall now reaches.

The King's Gate sits in the middle of the northern run of walls, which are mainly the work of 1296–1323. It was originally intended to be the main entrance to the castle but was never completed as such. Nevertheless, it demonstrates the immense strength of this most vulnerable part of the castle. It comprises a gate passage flanked by twin towers, with arrow loops and spy holes covering the approach. The passage was intended to be guarded by a drawbridge, six portsculli and five sets of doors, with murder holes in the ceiling to drop unpleasant items on heads or water to extinguish fires. Additionally there was a

The Chamberlain Tower, with the Queen's Tower behind, seen from the Black Tower. The Chamberlain Tower on the south side once joined to the King's Gate on the north, thus demarking the Upper Ward from the Lower Ward beyond. The stair on the wall head leads down to the first-floor wall passage visible to its right; originally this would have been roofed over. Another passage runs below it at ground level. The kink in the walls marks where they cross the old Norman motte.

right angle as the main passage turned into a smaller passage before passing over a second drawbridge into the Lower Ward. Passing the third portcullis slots, doors either side lead to the porters' lodges. The rear of the western twin tower extends back into the courtyard but very little remains of the eastern tower, which was barely started before work halted. In the western part a door leads to a stair rising to a first-floor wall passage, thence across the western tower to a chapel over the gate passage. Two of the portsculli rise into this room (a double piscina removes all doubt as to its purpose); this not only shows – as in some other castles – that the juxtaposition of defence and living was not necessarily the same to the medieval mind as to our own, but also that probably the portsculli were normally kept lowered. The wall passages at first-floor level have arrow loops that could in fact be used by twice as many archers. On the floor above a hall was planned to run across the whole area covered by the twin towers and chapel, but it was never finished. Above the outer doorway can be seen a stone statue of Edward II, placed there in 1321.

Moving westwards, the first mural tower is the Well Tower, but a kitchen range abutted the curtain wall between this and the King's Gate. The range, reduced now to foundations, was of three rooms, the westernmost having at its western end cavities for two large copper cauldrons and another cavity behind that may have been for smoking meat or fish. The Well Tower provided water that ran in lead piping in a channel behind the ovens, with a drain below it, while a second pipe ran along the curtain wall to feed a stone sink in the wall in the westernmost kitchen room. A wall outlet was provided in the curtain, leading to a vertical chute for rubbish disposal. The easternmost room had a door leading to a stair to a room above and also to the King's Gate.

The layout of the Well Tower mirrors that of most of the mural towers. It comprises four rooms, including a basement. The ground, first and second floors were each carried on timber floors, the joists' weight taken on two large cross beams fitting into holes in the wall, each additionally supported on a stone corbel. A fireplace served each floor together with a latrine reached via an outside wall passage. From the ground-floor entrance a passage runs around to the well chamber. The well is 15m (50ft) deep and was used to provide the water for a lead-lined cistern feeding the pipes sloping down to the kitchens. The shaft also continues up to the floor above with a mural chamber and fireplace. From this floor one could walk to the Eagle Tower beyond, whilst it was also intended that a walk ran from the floor above, but the curtain was never finished to this height. The Well Tower also had a basement entrance protected by a door. From this room an additional entrance from the ditch allowed supplies from ships or boats to be brought in for the kitchen. This vulnerable spot was guarded by doors on the outer and inner side, as well as a portcullis and murder holes. The Well Tower was never fully finished and today's ramparts and turret are of 19th-century build.

The town walls run from the Eagle Tower to the North-West Tower, a distance of approximately 734m (800 yards). On the south side there is no wall, but the town is separated from the castle by a ditch, which would have been twice as wide as it is now. On the west the walls were bounded by the Menai Strait, on the north and east sides by the River Cadnant.

The town defences would have started on the west from the Eagle Tower, from whose wall the springer for an arch and two doors above were intended to connect to the Water Gate. This would have been the entrance for water-borne traffic, but was never completed. The existing wall across from the castle dates from 1326 and was not part of Edward's layout, and the remains of a postern doorway now connect to a modern arch in the ditch. The wall then runs north and is set with eight mural towers and two gates, the latter on the west and east sides, connecting via a road across the town thus enclosed. The wall on this side was built early in the 14th century to replace the wooden quay that was destroyed during the uprising of 1294–95. The first and southernmost tower is of D-section, as are all but the northermost of these towers. Beyond the first tower is the West Gate, also called the Golden Gate, a passage flanked by twin D-shaped towers, and fronted by a small barbican. The portcullis grooves can be seen. The northernmost of its towers has a partially remaining latrine built out from the wall-walk, but the battlements and window openings are of 19th-century date. The next tower also has these later reconstructions together with a door and chimney of similar date. These towers cannot be explored internally but the view from the walkway beside the Menai Strait is less hampered by later additions than on the eastern wall section, where the town has sprawled beyond the confines of its walls. The northernmost tower protects the angle of the curtain as it turns east and is the only cylindrical tower. In the early 14th century St Mary's Chapel was built in this angle, of which work the arcades survive. The chapel utilized a postern arch that was moved several feet to form the west door. However, this obvious weak spot was later filled in and remains so today. The cylindrical tower was used as a vestry. Beyond can be seen on the inner side one of the wall stairs climbing to the wall-walk of the curtain.

The next tower has a well-preserved stone bridge on its inner side, which replaced the initial timber version; the tower beyond is in much poorer condition internally. The curtain between these two towers still has some of the whitening that covered it until the 1930s, while the section beyond is in good condition generally, with original battlements whose merlons have remains of arrow loops. Three modern openings breach the wall along this northern stretch

Caernarfon town wall seen from across the Menai Strait. The West, Water or Golden Gate is in the centre and the castle is out of picture to the right.

Caernarfon town walls seen from the western walls of the castle, with the Menai Strait to the left. In the foreground is the first mural tower beyond the Eagle Tower of the castle, with the West, Water or Golden Gate beyond it.

of curtain. An angle tower defines the change in direction to a more southerly run of curtain, this tower having original battlements retaining remains of finials on their crestings. Beyond this tower is another internal wall stair leading to the curtain wall-walk. Running south-east, the East Gate, also known as the Great or Exchequer Gate, is reached. The main landward entrance, it consists of twin D-shaped towers flanking the gate passage. The rooms above the gate were used for the Exchequer. Latterly much of the top part of the gate was altered or lost. A drawbridge originally guarded the approach across a timber bridge, the latter replaced after the revolt of 1294–95 by a stone, five-arched bridge across the River Cadnant, built in 1301 or 1302. Today the little river is culverted over and the drawbridge was replaced by a stone arch at some time after 1520. Part of the original bridge has been exposed. In front of the main gate was a smaller, lower gateway connected to the main gate by a drawbridge. It served as a focal point for mercantile toll collection.

The curtain wall beyond the gate has been refaced with a pink stone. The next mural tower survives to its battlements and is flanked by remains of the revetment constructed to hold the banks at the base of the walls. An alleyway in Hole in the Wall Street gives a view of the inside of this tower. The curtain from this tower runs south-westerly to the final tower, whose inside is now bare save for a line of putlog holes rising at an angle. Immediately beyond is a small postern, the Green Gate, so-called from the castle green (now Castle Square) beyond. The postern was originally defended by doors and a portcullis. Here also is another of the curtain wall stairs that led to the wall-walk. The curtain then runs along to meet the castle at the North-East Tower.

Life in the castles

Royal castles had to be capable of sustaining not only military forces that might gather there but also the king and queen with all their entourage, which itself might number 350 people. As Prince Edward grew, he too might require housing.

Since such castles took years to complete they also had to cater for the builders working on them or on adjacent town walls. All this required adequate supplies and storage facilities and an efficient method of bringing provisions into the castle. A number of castles built near the sea or on rivers were provided with walls and gates that opened onto a quayside. Rhuddlan had a Dock Gate next to the square Gillot's Tower on the outer curtain; at high tide the River Clwyd flowed into the moat by the dock. At Harlech a path led down the rock from the outer curtain – the 'Way from the Sea' – protected by a wall; a turret with drawbridge barred the way down to the Water Gate, also with a drawbridge. Beaumaris had a 'Gate next the Sea' (the main entrance in the southern outer curtain) near a defended dock with a mill that jutted out into the water.

Castles actually spent much of the time at peace. Many consist of two wards, the outer of which, with direct access to the main gate, was the hub of the castle's everyday life and contained service buildings and workshops, sometimes even beyond the walls. Many such structures have long gone; there are no internal buildings now at Beaumaris, Flint or Rhuddlan but some were timber lean-tos, others houses, while some workshops were within towers. Stables were vital, for warhorses, riding horses and draught horses, probably often with an upper floor for hay and sleeping quarters for the grooms. There would be other animal pens and sometimes a dovecot, like the square example at Denbigh, for fresh meat. There might also be kennels for hunting dogs. A mill for grinding corn was common, sometimes a windmill or water mill but often a hand mill. The inner ward at Conwy housed a granary, while at Harlech it is set against the south curtain and sits on a slightly raised floor above a low basement. The Bakehouse Tower at Conwy is so-named since it has an oven built into the thickness of the wall. A brewhouse produced beer, the process of which killed germs found in well water. Workshops were necessary for smiths, carpenters, armourers etc. At

Conwy castle, begun in March 1283, from the north, showing the west barbican at the extreme left. The path is modern; originally entry was via a drawbridge spanning the pit in front of the small barbican bastions.

The west barbican at Conwy shielded the entrance into the castle proper. Behind the barbican, the two towers either side were fitted to the outline of the rock rather than set close beside the gate passage. The town wall at far right runs down to join the castle.

Harlech the North-West Tower was known as the 'Armourer's Tower' in the 1564 survey, possibly a throwback to when the 'artiller', mentioned in 1284, had his workshop there. Rhuddlan had an outer ward at least 18m (60ft) wide on three sides, where might have been sited the great and little stables, a granary, a forge, a workshop for the queen's goldsmith and even the treasury. There were also shelters under which stood engines for defence of the castle, one of which faced the River Clwyd. In 1303 round stones were bought from Gwespyr and cut to shape by Robert of Melbourne, a Derbyshire mason. The inner ward had timber buildings against the inside of the walls, running to the gatehouses where they met a timber gate structure butting the rear of the gate passage.

OPPOSITE **The living site: Conwy**

The Inner Ward at Conwy (shown in plan view, 1) was laid out with three private rooms on the first floor. The central (top corner) room (2) was (according to a 1627 survey) the Presence Chamber of the king and queen. It abutted the large cylindrical south-east corner mural tower, with a bed chamber on two floors (possibly for the king and queen). To the north was the Great Chamber (3), reached via an external staircase. It contained fine traceried windows, those on the outer side overlooking the garden laid out in the East Barbican (4). In addition, a door in the north-east angle led into the cylindrical corner tower where there was a chapel, a useful adjunct to ceremonial functions. The Great Chamber connected to the Presence Chamber by a door. From the other side of this room a door led into the Privy Chamber, the smaller of the two outer chambers, with a small room, probably a lobby, beyond. Below this level (according to the 1627 survey) was an arched cellar under the Great Chamber, a kitchen under the Presence Chamber and a Parlour under the Privy Chamber.

A stair led from the Presence Chamber through the curtain to the private garden in the East Barbican (4), this reconstruction based on the surviving illustration of c.1600.

The monarch could leave the castle via stairs to a small private water gate. Access was also viable from the barbican up to the Great Chamber. Flower beds in these rather formal gardens tended to be raised alongside paths, with trellises and raised benches of sods. Gardens often contained herbs used for cooking and medicine, and vines.

The ground-floor hall at Conwy (5) is partly formed from the curtain wall and so follows its line. Beyond was a chapel, separated from the hall by a timber-framed partition, as was a smaller hall at the other end. The northern part of the complex stood on the rock but the southern half had a timber floor over a long, narrow cellar. The chevron pattern of painted plasterwork is unconfirmed but based on Savoyard designs.

The Prison Tower at Conwy (6). A passage from a window embrasure in the great hall led through a doorway and thence off a tower stair down some steps to an opening into the tower with a 1.2m (4ft) drop to a wooden floor on beams. From here a trapdoor would have accessed a smooth-sided pit with a single narrow ventilation shaft.

Also shown are a cutaway of one of the projecting latrines on the town wall at Conwy (7) and a plan view of the castle and town walls (8).

Looking down from the inner ward on to the hall complex in the outer ward of Conwy. Half the hall is provided with a narrow cellar. The stone arch is a 14th-century addition replacing the original wooden structures. Note the continuous route round the towers from the wall-walk.

A well was essential in case of siege. At Rhuddlan it is some 50ft (15m) deep while that at Conwy (70ft/21.7m deep) was originally fitted with a lid and set in a well house, as evidenced by a 16th-century drawing. A tank had to be brought up temporarily to Hope castle after the Welsh blocked the well with stones. Cisterns were also employed in castles; Criccieth has one at one side of the gatehouse passage, fed by a spring and rebated for a wooden cover at ground level. The cistern at Caernarfon was set in a stone-lined tank on top of the aptly named Cistern Tower, for collecting rainwater.

The preference during the 13th century for square or rectangular forms of castle meant that domestic buildings adapted to this format. At Harlech the great hall is placed against the west wall, opposite the great gatehouse on the east. The southern end of the hall opens into the kitchen via screens, a buttery and pantry. These elements take up the whole western side, with a covered pentise running along the outer side (three corbels for its roof survive on the kitchen wall). From the head of the hall a right turn led along the north side to the chapel (some white internal plastering survives), with a bakehouse beyond. Against the south wall lay a second hall with a granary beyond, the latter over a low basement (floor-beam slots in the curtain point out the raised floor). The second hall may have been a timber-framed hall that was dismantled and rebuilt in the castle almost as a sign of dominance. It has been suggested that the domestic layout and shape at Harlech was then influential in less martial 14th-century courtyard houses, but the regular design was by no means universal in contemporary castles. At Beaumaris there are opposed gatehouses to the north and south, so the hall (with low basement and chamber above) runs along the east wall, with perhaps kitchen and stables opposite on the west wall. Near the hall there is an oven in the angle formed by the north curtain and south-east stair turret of the North Gatehouse. The inner ward of Rhuddlan may have had two halls against the inner walls set either side of a kitchen in the northern angle, with chambers at the further ends. The timber supports of the overhang of the upper floor apartments seem to have formed a colonnaded passage below. Records show that their roofs were of shingle. At Criccieth the wall-walk of the south-west and western sections of inner curtain is cut by channels, drains voiding through holes in the parapet to remove water from the eaves of a hall presumably built against the inner side.

Large ground-floor halls are found at Caernarfon and Conwy, some 25–30m in length. Both are placed against the curtain wall, being in the lower ward at Caernarfon and the outer ward at Conwy. As the main area of each castle, these halls were obviously intended for the use of the garrison and others. At Conwy, however, the inner ward was palpably the domain of the royal family and was deliberately laid out to make the most of the fact, with three main interconnecting rooms at first-floor level, set along the south and east sides so as to make a right angle, all complete with fireplaces.

In several of Edward's castles the great gatehouses also carried residential rooms. The two upper floors at Harlech each had a large hall or chamber, plus a smaller chamber, unequally divided; a chapel stood over the gate passage. It has been suggested that James of St George had his residence in this gatehouse, since he was constable in 1290. There is no chamber block in the hall complex beyond and the kitchen along the courtyard wall could have served both hall and gatehouse quarters. The upper suite is likely to have been for the king or other visitors of rank. Beaumaris had a very similar arrangement but was intended to be even larger, as far as can be surmised from the surviving incomplete work (especially in the South Gatehouse). The North Gatehouse had a first-floor hall measuring some 21m × 7.5m (70ft × 25ft), although it was probably intended to be unequally divided by a cross-wall – as at Harlech – and had five large and attractive windows facing into the courtyard; had the building been completed there would have been another five for the missing floor above. Together with the hall and chamber in the courtyard, the castle would have had five suites of rooms (plus 19 rooms if all the towers of the inner ward are included), perhaps built with an eye to the future family and household of the young Prince of Wales, not to mention his father.

The cross-wall dividing the two wards, seen from the outer ward of Conwy. At its foot is the remains of the wall protecting the well.

However, it should not be supposed that this castle, or any other, would have regularly teemed with knights, nobles and royalty. Despite the elaborate Inner Ward at Conwy, King Edward only visited it once, in the winter of 1294/95 during the uprising of Madog; no royal visitor came again until Richard II in 1399, shortly before his deposition. In 1277, nine mounted serjeants and 40 foot soldiers protected the castle at Builth, though after the surrender of Llewelyn it was reduced to four horsemen and ten infantry. After the revolt of 1294 Builth tended to become a muster point, and men grouped there for service abroad in 1319, 1321, 1334 and 1385. In 1284 Conwy had a constable who had to answer for state prisoners and was also ex officio mayor. He controlled 30 'fencible men' of whom 15 were crossbowmen; the rest were watchmen, porters and servants. The castle was also home to a chaplain, mason, carpenter, smith and armourer.

A chapel was normally included in the castle. At Harlech it is set against the north wall at an angle to the north end of the great hall; it had a lean-to roof but with a ceiling masking it off internally, where some white internal plastering survives on the west wall. The great hall in the outer ward at Conwy similarly had a chapel set at the eastern end of the great hall and separated off by timber-framed partitions. Other chapels were more private. One of the earliest was at Flint, with its barrel-vaulted chapel in the upper floor of the great circular tower, being one of the rooms surrounding the central apartment. At Conwy and Beaumaris a royal chapel is on the first floor of the circular Chapel

The private apartments of the inner ward at Conwy. Next to the cross wall and King's Tower (far right) is a small lobby, with the Privy Chamber next to it; the arch is a 14th-century addition. The Presence Chamber is on the extreme left, joined at right-angles by the wall of the Great Chamber.

Tower, the former in the north-east corner of the inner ward (entered from the Great chamber), the latter on the east side of the inner ward (probably entered via an arched doorway from the lost range likely to have been the main residential suite). At Conwy the chancel was formed from a recess ending in an apse, cut into the wall thickness. This was arcaded in seven bays in two tiers, three upper tiers being pierced by lancet windows. The ends of the lower arcade may have once held a rood beam with a figure of Christ. A stair at the entrance led up to a small private viewing chamber. At Beaumaris, in an angle between the Chapel Tower and the outer side of the inner curtain wall, there is a small projection carried on corbels that might have been for a bell, rather like one at Rhuddlan. The great gatehouses utilized the small room on the floors over the passage for private chapels, as mentioned in connection with Beaumaris and Harlech (where a mural chamber each side acted as a vestry).

Shields were sometimes hung over the battlements for show. Bordeaux supplied 200 'targeis' in 1287–88, complete with the royal arms, for the king's castles in Wales, while 100 rounded boards were brought to Rhuddlan to make shields for Gillot's Tower and the gate towards the Clywd in 1304, together with fixing pieces. Here too 64 shillings was paid in 1283 for four pieces of red silk for royal pennons and standards. Interior walls were usually plastered and some rooms – especially the royal chambers – were painted, as at Rhuddlan in 1282–83 for the queen's visit. Here some wood was specially brought from Gascony for the 'queen's work', which included a camera (private room) and her goldsmith's building. Large windows were fitted with iron stanchions and might be barred externally to keep undesirables out. Timber floors were plastered or cemented, and often painted or tiled; floors were covered with rushes, probably woven into mats, which were changed in spring. Braziers were used where fireplaces were absent.

Bodily comfort was not forgotten. The triple-towered gatehouse at Denbigh has five garderobes in the north-west tower that all empty into a common cesspit. At Conwy the section of town wall west of Mill Gate is very unusual in having 12 small privvies corbelled out from the wall-head (at a cost of £15 in 1286). Conwy and Caernarfon have latrines on the curtain walls, set in the thickness. Chamber pots would be common.

Perhaps surpisingly it is often difficult to pinpoint precise buildings used for housing prisoners awaiting sentence or ransom. Some could simply be held in a convenient tower, while men of rank might be housed in decent conditions. However, the cylindrical North-East Tower at Harlech has a deep basement chamber that was reached only via a trap door in the floor and was lit and ventilated by a single narrow shaft rising sharply to the outside. Since the floor has long since gone it is possible that the access hatch was quite wide or even had a winch for moving stores but, as it is called the Prison Tower in the 1343 survey, it seems likely that it was indeed used to incarcerate prisoners. However, it should be noted that the South-East Tower has a very similar basement but was called the Garden Tower in the survey.

Formal gardens were sometimes a feature of castle life. The Inner Ward at Conwy looked out on the garden planted in the East Barbican, while a formal garden was in existence by the 16th century beyond the castle, outside the southern part of the town wall. Lawns tended to have rather long grass containing wild flowers. In Rhuddlan castle 6,000 turfs were laid to lawn in the courtyard in 1282, with a fence of used cask staves. Adjacent to this the roofed well had a fishpond around its head surrounded with seats, the pond lined with four cartloads of clay from the marsh. A lawn was created within Caernarfon when only the temporary timber buildings stood, and a swan's nest was to be made in the middle of the millpond there.

The view from the inner ward at Conwy over the cross-wall to the outer ward, with the windows of the great hall visible, and foundations of the kitchens and stable block on the right.

The castles at war

There were obvious problems in manoeuvring siege equipment in the native terrain. In August 1287 Edmund of Cornwall brought 4,000 men out of Carmarthen, to be joined by Reginald Grey from Chester and Roger L'Estrange from Montgomery with 6,700, to besiege the rebel Rhys of Dryslwyn in Dryslwyn castle. A great machine was used, probably a trebuchet. This required four-wheeled wains pulled by 40 oxen, with another 20 over rough country; 20 horsemen and 450 footsoldiers acted as escort. Stone balls were brought by 20 quarrymen and 24 carters, 480 being carried by a train of packhorses (two balls over 16in. in diameter have been discovered during excavations). The siege lasted for 20 days, during which miners accidentally brought down a section of wall prematurely, killing some of their own knights including the Earl of Stafford. Although the castle had fallen by 5 September, Rhys escaped and in November seized Emlyn castle in a surprise attack.

As we have seen, some of these castles were partly or wholly rebuilt and occupied by English troops. Carreg Cennen (also known as Caer Cynan), for example, was captured in 1277 by a Marcher baron, Pain de Chaworth. It was dismantled after 1282 but was repaired not long afterwards by the Earl of Gloucester, who then filled it with 500 men. Rhys of Dryslwyn took it but soon lost it again. It was then held by the castellan, John Skidmore, who kept it for over a year against the Welsh besiegers when the rest of Carmarthenshire had been lost.

So strong were the castles built by Edward I that they were extremely difficult to capture. The best chance of success open to the Welsh was to storm them whilst they were being built. Once completed they presented formidable obstacles, the best option then being to blockade them. However, the sea or river sites commonly chosen reaped dividends; provided such lines of communication could be kept open, supply vessels could bring food, weapons and men into a beleaguered stronghold under the noses of the besiegers. Moreover, the king used a policy of road building to link the castles and ease lines of communication. The feared mine, silent and deadly, could be rendered useless by the rocky foundations chosen by the designers. It was the use of competent gunpowder artillery that perhaps proved the main threat to such fortifications, but this came over a century after they had been built.

Despite their strength it was noted that during the revolt of 1287 castles were weakly manned, assisting the capture of Dinefwr, Carreg Cennen, and Llandovery. In 1294 Madog ap Llywelyn, a cousin of the last Welsh prince, led a revolt against the English in Wales but especially in the north. Some of the castles had no castellan since troops, including Welsh levies, had been drawn off for an expedition to Gascony. Caernarfon was attacked, the new town walls were badly damaged and the sheriff killed. The Welsh then charged the wooden bretagium and continued across the moat into the castle, which was only partly built. Everything that could burn was set on fire, including the records held there. Edward demanded that the town be back at readiness by 11 November 1295. By summer the Welsh had been pushed back and the town walls of Caernarfon had been rebuilt at high speed, being finished two months ahead of this target date. Edward appears to have decided that it was the castle walls opposite the town that were the most important and once repaired it was this section that seems to have received the most serious attention. The same uprising also saw the castle at Builth attacked. In the winter of 1294 the besieged garrison there consisted of three heavy and three light horsemen,

20 crossbowmen and 40 archers. The force that came to their assistance was composed of 10 knights, 20 heavy and 40 light horse, but they came up against stiff resistance. They had to make five attempts before they managed to break through the siege lines. Thus the castle was relieved, unlike those at Cefnllys and Morlais to the north and south. Cardigan, Bere and Denbigh were also besieged. The latter was captured but Flint and Rhuddlan held out without too much difficulty. The constable of Flint was also the mayor, and burnt the town to deny cover and food to the enemy. Harlech resisted the rebels with a garrison of only 20 men. It was cut off by land together with the castles of Llanbadarn (Aberystwyth) and Criccieth but all continued to be supplied by sea from Ireland and successfully defied the rebels. On arrival at Chester, Edward found troops at Rhuddlan to swell the English army and soon Ruthin and Denbigh had been purged of rebels. Unfortunately for him, on moving from Conwy towards Bangor early in January, the royal baggage train was set upon and seized. However, Madog was defeated in battle at Maes Moydog on 5 March 1295 and soon after gave in. In both the 1287 and 1294 revolts, many Welshmen had fought on Edward's side, which undermined the attempts from the start.

Even obviously powerful fortifications might receive further attention, prompted by an enemy attack. Once the siege of Harlech was over, the castle was reinforced by the building of a stone and lime wall to enclose the steep rock face on the north side, with a tower protecting the Water Gate. Further reinforcement came in 1323–24 during the reign of Edward II when two rectangular towers were raised in the ditch in front of the main gate, the towers in a line connected by a stone-arched bridge, with a drawbridge at each end, according to a Tudor description.

It was in the 15th century that some of Edward's castles found themselves in the firing line once more, this time literally, for gunpowder was beginning to make itself felt in siege warfare. Between 1400 and c.1413 Owain Glyn Dŵr led a national uprising against the English. In September 1400 the town of Rhuddlan was attacked but the castle held out and the rebels were rebuffed. Criccieth was put on alert, but Conwy was captured in 1401. There had already been work done in 1384–86 and 1388–90 in which bridges had been repaired (apparently on the walls or towers); now further repairs were done. By spring 1402 the

Rhuddlan was another of Edward's fortresses, started in August 1277 as a result of his invasion that year. The twin-towered West Gatehouse of the Inner Ward stands on the left. The square tower down on the right is Gillot's Tower, with the River Wall to its left, running to the River Gate.

The siege of Rhuddlan, 1282

54

garrison consisted of a man-at-arms and 11 (later 12) bowmen; the one received double the pay of the others. Soon the constable was allowed to upgrade the garrison to six men-at-arms and 50 archers at £416 14s 2d per year – similar to that of Harlech's garrison, which had long been under siege. These castles could be reinforced by sea from Caernarfon or Conwy, but in the autumn of 1403–04 a French and Breton fleet arrived in the Irish Sea to support the Welsh. Caernarfon held out when besieged in 1403 and 1404, its garrison down to 28 men, causing casualties of 300 amongst the besiegers. Beaumaris, Harlech and Aberystwyth castles were besieged and the latter two fell in the spring of 1404 after long battles against starvation. Harlech had put up a brave front, holding out for many months until its garrison was down to 21; Criccieth followed. Owain placed his family and his court in Harlech. He may also have been formally crowned as prince of Wales in the castle. Glyn Dŵr gave it a garrison under Edmund Mortimer, who found himself besieged in turn as Glyn Dŵr's forces were pushed back and into the hills. In 1408 an English army under Henry of Monmouth, the future Henry V, arrived at Harlech. However, the living rock

The ruined remains of the North Tower in the inner ward at Rhuddlan.

OPPOSITE **The siege of Rhuddlan, 1282**

During the Welsh uprising of 1282 Llywelyn marched on Rhuddlan and on the first day, 22 March, attacked the town. It was defended by a timber (as opposed to a stone) palisade and even this was probably unfinished. The castle had been completed but the rebels turned their attention to it, probably the same day. Catapults were brought up to bombard it and lead from Northop, bound for the castle at Flint, was seized and sent to Rhuddlan for the catapults there. The siege dragged on for a month but it is not known for certain if the castle was actually captured. If so, the rebels' success was brief. A relief force under Amadeus of Savoy, the king's cousin, had set out from Chester on 21 April and was

approaching; the Welsh decided to withdraw. Certainly significant damage must have been sustained, as is witnessed from the repairs carried out. Already in June timber from Delamere Forest was being organized, probably to remedy the defects in the town defences, rather than to repair any damage; 20 carts transported it from the riverside on arrival in August. However, further supplies were diverted to the works at Caernarfon in 1283. Edward made Rhuddlan his headquarters from July 1282 until the following March (when he moved to Conwy), and for over two years further work was carried out. A plan view of the castle and town is provided at bottom right.

was a huge obstacle to mining. Henry proceeded to bombard it with cannon fire. A heap of stone balls survive on the floor of the gatehouse and may testify to this event, as may the loss of much of the outer curtain on the south and east sides. This was the main side on which artillery might have been sited, other sides presenting a sheer drop that made access to batteries difficult. One of the guns, called the 'King's Daughter', burst during firing. Castles in Britain were generally slower in adapting to artillery than on the continent, probably due to the fact that warfare was less common. Notwithstanding, the siege of Harlech continued, though details of other methods of attack are not forthcoming: perhaps it was too strong to contemplate them.

Henry left the Talbots to deal with Harlech, and marched to Aberystwyth. The garrison agreed they would yield after a set period if not relieved, so Henry, calculating that no help would come, left during the winter months. However, Glyn Dŵr got in and rallied the garrison, so a rejuvenated enemy awaited Henry on his return. At Aberystwyth Henry used mines and 'all manner of engines' to accomplish his victory against Glyn Dŵr's garrison, who gave up in the late summer of 1408. At Harlech, the blockade began to bite. The castle started to suffer a shortage of food and no provisions were forthcoming by sea. By the end of the year or early in 1409 there was a critical lack of food in Harlech and Mortimer, along with many of his garrison, died of exhaustion. The castle succumbed too and it was retaken.

Even in the Wars of the Roses, most conflict by far took the form of battles in the open field. Sieges were few, and the two battles of St Albans involved assaults on defended positions in the town as opposed to an attack on an existing fortress. However, some activity did occur around castles. In 1460 Harlech had given refuge to Henry VI's queen, Margaret of Anjou. From 1461 a Welsh constable, Dafydd ap Ievan ap Einion, held Harlech for the Lancastrians. In 1468 the castle was besieged by the Yorkist William Herbert, Earl of Pembroke, and his brother, Sir Richard Herbert of Coldbrook, their two forces of 7–10,000 men converging on it. Many guns and bows were used in the action, and the defenders held out for less than a month. Harlech was surrendered on 14 August 1468 after seven years in Lancastrian hands. The garrison was allowed to leave unharmed. The song 'Men of Harlech' supposedly refers to this siege. It was said of Dafydd: 'He had once in his youth maintained a castle so long in France that every old woman in Wales had heard of it, and in his old age had held a castle in Wales so long that every old woman in France had heard of it.'

Even in the 17th century Edwardian castles were being held mainly against Parliament, but time had moved on and, despite gallant resistance, improved gunpowder made them appear what they had become – antique structures in a modern world.

Aftermath

Already in the 14th century, some of Edward I's castles were falling into disrepair. With Wales at peace their massive strength was a rather costly burden. Caernarfon and Beaumaris had never been fully built. In 1322 it was reported that the castles were ruinous and 'not fit' for the king to visit. Conwy, neglected like several others, had rotten trusses in the hall because the roof was neglected.

However, during the Wars of the Roses some of the castles provided useful strongholds for the factions supporting York or Lancaster. The accession in 1485 of Henry Tudor as Henry VII saw a king with Welsh blood now ruling England. A sympathy with Welsh views was established and some 50 years later the government of Wales was partly assimilated with that of England. Already in 1539 a report by Crown surveyors shows that Conwy, Caernarfon and Harlech could not be defended for a single hour in the event of a French or Scottish invasion. The Tudors had brought the means for peaceful co-existence and lessened the need for fortresses in Wales. This led to many being neglected and becoming ruinous; roof leadwork was ignored and so water and damp seeped in, leading to timbers rotting and ultimately to roofs collapsing. Builth was in decay and the whole castle was demolished during the second half of the 16th century so that the materials could be used again. A survey of 1564 shows that the interior of nearly every tower in Harlech was 'in utter ruin', while the hall and chapel were roofless; the drawbridges had been replaced by wooden constructions that were themselves rotting.

Leland, who travelled across England and Wales between 1535 and 1545, noted in his *Itinerary* the state of castles, in which he was particularly interested; however, his work is difficult to use. Despite the decay the castles were still powerful strongpoints and in the Civil Wars of the 17th century were seen as

Probably built between 1282 and 1329 for Roger Mortimer, Chirk castle has been continually occupied. The tops of the towers may never have been completed.

Montgomery castle, a base in the Marches held by the Mortimer family. The Inner War of c. 1224 can be seen beyond the Middle War of c. 1251–53. The left-hand tower fragment is late 13th–14th-century work.

such. The Welsh squirarchy had, under the Tudors, become more loyal to the monarchy and tended to hold castles for the king. Caernarfon was garrisoned and besieged three times. Rhuddlan held out until July 1646 before surrendering to Thomas Mytton, being slighted two years later. On 15 March 1647 Harlech's royalist garrison of 14 gentlemen and 28 men surrendered to Mytton, signifying the end of the Civil War.

In the mid 17th century, following the execution of Charles I, many castles were slighted by Parliament to make them untenable, a procedure more common in Wales and western England than elsewhere, partly because the Irish threat had been confronted. Beaumaris, Caernarfon and Conwy, being on the coast, were given garrisons. Between 1646 and 1651 Conwy had platforms for its guns added or repaired. Other coastal castles were not so fortunate. Cardigan, Aberystwyth, Flint and perhaps Harlech were slighted and this was also the fate of many marcher strongholds. Flint was so well dismantled in 1652, following a change of hands several times, that it was described as almost buried in its own ruins. In 1655 Caernarfon and Conwy were ordered to be slighted; the breach in the Bakehouse Tower at Conwy was almost certainly done by gunpowder. When Charles II was restored in 1660 the process continued, as witnessed at Denbigh and Beaumaris; the same treatment was in store for Caernarfon but it proved half-hearted. Conwy had its roofs, lead, timber and iron torn out in 1665 and so was made uninhabitable. As at Rhuddlan, castles became convenient quarries for building materials. Holt was demolished between 1675 and 1683 so that Eaton Hall could be built.

The Victorians became more aware of castle ruins as romantic icons or of historical interest. Also, Welsh towns became more focused on the world beyond the borders. At Caernarfon the expansion of the slate industry opened up the place and a pride in its important ruin saw repairs undertaken in the last quarter of the century. In 1969 it became the centre of attention when Queen Elizabeth II held the much publicized investiture of her eldest son, Prince Charles, in the castle.

Visiting the castles today

Aberystwyth (Llanbadarn), Ceredigion
On the west coast on the A487 and A44. The ruins of the castle stand in the town near the New Promenade near the sea.

Beaumaris (Biwmaris), Isle of Anglesey (CADW)
Beaumaris lies some five miles north-east of the Menai Bridge, at the junction of the A545 and B5109. Unlike many of Edward's major castles it is low-lying. It was never completed.

Builth Wells, Powys
At the junction of the A470 and A483. A path near the Lion Hotel leads to the castle, which has been reduced to earthworks alone.

Caernarfon, Gwynedd (CADW)
On the A487, about 10 miles south-west of Bangor. The massive castle is hard to miss, sitting in the town with the Menai Strait on one side and the fortified town walls on the other.

Cardigan (Aberteifi), Ceredigion (private)
On the A487, the castle walls can only be viewed from the outside when approaching the town, which means avoiding the by-pass.

Carmarthen (Caerfyrddin), Carmarthenshire
On the A40. The ruins stand in the middle of the town.

Carndochan, Gwynedd
The castle ruins are located off the A494 near Bala.

Carreg Cennen, Carmarthenshire (CADW)
Three miles north of Ammanford on the A483, turn east at Llandybie. The castle is set imposingly on a crag in the Black Mountain Forest.

Castell y Bere, Gwynedd (CADW)
Off the B4405 about two miles from Abergynolwyn, and south-west of Llanfihangel-y-pennant. The ruinous castle sits surrounded by trees on an outcrop below Cadair Idris in the Dysynni valley.

Ruthin castle is now partly absorbed into a modern hotel.

Chirk (Castell y Waun), Wrexham (National Trust)

Six miles north of Oswestry on the A483, turn west on to the B4500. Unlike most others listed here it is still partly occupied; it is roofed and contains later room settings.

Conwy, Conwy (CADW)

At the mouth of the River Conwy, the town is on the A547, from which junction the B5106 runs south down the Vale of Conwy. The view of the castle is partly spoiled by Telford's Victorian railway bridge at the east end and railway lines running alongside. The town walls are among the best preserved in Britain and repay a visit; begin from the castle by walking through the arch to the north-east, and walk around the town walls and up Mount Pleasant to reach Tower 13 on the far south-west of the town walls, for a view of the castle. Then pass under the Upper Gate into Rosemary Lane and then Rose Hill Street, for an internal view on the return journey to the castle.

Criccieth, Gwynedd (CADW)

On the A497 about five miles west of Porthmadog. The castle is sited on a rocky promontory by the sea, to the south side of the town. The path from the ticket office climbs the slope but turns right instead of left, which it did originally to meet the outer gatehouse, a route no longer feasible because of later quarrying of the cliff on this side.

Denbigh (Dinbych), Denbighshire (CADW)

To the south of Denbigh on the B4501 and A543, in the Vale of Clwyd. The castle is set on a rocky outcrop by the town. The town walls join the castle north-west

A plan view of Ruthin castle. (Adam Hook)

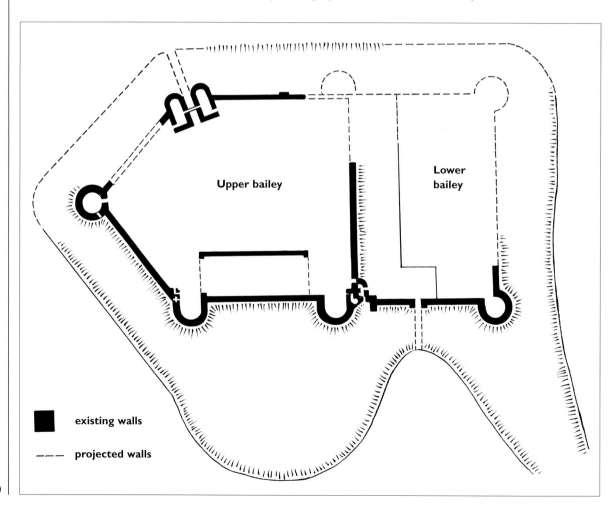

Upper bailey

Lower bailey

■ existing walls

- - - projected walls

of the great gatehouse and can be accessed. The best section is that including the Goblin Tower, beyond Lord Leicester's church on the far north-east side. There are also the ruins of the late 13th-century friary to visit.

Dinas Brân, Denbighshire
The ruins are located off the A539 north-east of Llangollen.

Dinefwr, Carmarthenshire (CADW)
From Llandeilo off the A483, the castle ruins are situated one mile west of the town.

Dolbadarn, Gwynedd (CADW)
On the A4086, nine and a half miles south-east of Caernarfon. The ruins are located on a rocky outcrop in the Llanberis Pass.

Dolforwyn, Powys (CADW)
The ruins stand on a hill near Abermule, off the A483.

Dolwyddelan, Conwy (CADW)
From the A470, the castle is on a hill on the slopes of Moel Siabod, about 5 miles north of Blaenau Ffestiniog.

Dryslwyn, Carmarthenshire (CADW)
On the B4297, five miles west of Llandeilo. Ruinous, a few pieces of wall and earthworks survive.

Ewloe, Flintshire (CADW)
Half a mile north-west of Ewloe on the B5125, the castle ruins are set within woodland in Wepre Park, reached by walking through the fields.

Flint (Y Fflint), Flintshire (CADW)
Ten miles north-west of Chester in the centre of Flint, reached via the A548 running along the river or the A5119 from Mold. It is the least well preserved of Edward's major castles. The outer ditch originally extended to what is now Castle Dyke Street and it is worth entering the castle via this route, which traces the path across what would have been the timber bridge.

Harlech, Gwynedd (CADW)
East of the A496 in the centre of town, about 11 miles north of Barmouth. The castle is set on a promontory. It is worth descending the steps to the Water Gate near the railway station at the base of the rock, to see the majesty of the castle rising on its natural defences above.

Haverford (Hwlffordd), Pembrokeshire
In the centre of Haverfordwest, on the A40, A487, and A4076.

Hawarden, Flintshire
At the junction of the A550 and B5125. A stone archway in the centre of the town gives access to the wooded park of Ewart Gladstone's mansion, within which is the castle, the most prominent remains being a great circular tower standing on a mound.

Holt, Wrexham
At the junction of the B5102 and B5130, close to the A534 about four miles east of Wrexham. The low-lying ruins have suffered since much of the stonework was taken in the 17th century but some remains, partly obscured by vegetation.

Hope (Caergwrle), Flintshire
On the A541, about five miles north west of Wrexham on a hill above Caergwrle, much of the castle has gone but walls on the south and east sides remain.

Montgomery (Trefaldwyn), Powys (CADW)
At the junction of the B4385, B4386 and B4388, about six miles south of Welshpool. Access is by Castle Hill in the town.

Rhuddlan, Denbighshire (CADW)
On the A547, about two miles south of Rhyl, the castle lies on the southern end of the town, on the River Clwyd.

Ruthin (Rhuthun), Denbighshire
On the A494 and A525, about seven miles south-east of Denbigh. In 1826 a house was built in the south-east part of the castle ruins. They now form part of a hotel.

Bibliography

In addition to the works cited, excellent guide books are available for many Edwardian castles from CADW, the agency responsible for protecting historic monuments in Wales.

Avent, Richard *Cestyll Tywysogion Gwynedd – Castles of the Princes of Gwynedd* (Cardiff, 1983).

Beresford, M. *New Towns of the Middle Ages* (London, 1967).

Brown, Allen R. *English Castles* (second edition, London, 1976).

Brown, Allen R. *Castles from the Air* (Cambridge, 1989).

Colvin, H.M., Brown, R.A. and Taylor, A.J. (eds.) *The History of the King's Works, The Middle Ages*, 2 vols (HMSO, London, 1963).

Davies, R.R. *Conquest, Coexistence, and Change: Wales 1063–1415* (Oxford, 1987), reprinted in paperback as *The Age of Conquest: Wales 1063–1415* (Oxford, 1991).

Davies, R.R. *The Revolt of Owain Glyn Dŵr* (Oxford, 1995).

Davis, A. 'Aberystwyth Castle', *Archaeology Wales* 25, pp.35–36.

Davis, A. 'Aberystwyth Castle', *Archaeology Wales* 26, pp.51–52.

Edwards, G. 'Edward I's Castle Building in Wales', *Proceedings of the British Academy*, 32 (1946), 15–81.

Gies, Joseph and Gies, Frances *Life in a Medieval Castle* (London, 1975).

Humphries, Peter *Castles of Edward I in Wales* (HMSO, 1983).

Jones, G.R.J. 'The Defences of Gwynedd in the Thirteenth Century', *Transactions of the Caernarvonshire Historical Society*, 30 (1969), 29–433.

Kenyon, J.R. *Medieval Fortifications* (Leicester University Press, 1990).

Kenyon, J.R. and Avent, R. (eds.) *Castles in Wales and the Marches; Essays in honour of D.J. Cathcart King* (University of Wales, Cardiff, 1987).

King, D.J.C. *The Castle in England and Wales* (Croom Helm, 1988).

King, D.J.C. 'The defence of Wales', *Archaeologia Cambrensis*, vol. 126, 1977, pp.1–16.

King, D.J.C. 'The Donjon of Flint', *Journal of the Chester and North Wales Architectural, Archaeological and Historical Society*, 45 (1958), 61–69.

Labarge, M.W. *The Baronial Household in the Thirteenth Century* (Brighton, 1980).

McNeill, Tom *Castles* (B.T. Batsford/English Heritage, London, 1992).

Morris, John E. *The Welsh Wars of Edward I* (reprinted, Stroud, 1997).

Neaverson, E. *Medieval Castles in North Wales: A Study of Sites, Water Supply and Building Stones* (Liverpool University Press, 1947).

Parker, Mike and Whitfield, Paul *Wales – The Rough Guide*, (Rough Guides Ltd, London, 1994).

Pettifer, Adrian *Welsh Castles: A Guide by Counties* (The Boydell Press, 2000).

Platt, Colin *The Castle in Medieval England and Wales* (Secker & Warburg, 1982).

Pounds, N.J.G. *The Medieval Castle in England and Wales* (Cambridge University Press, 1994).

Prestwich, M. *Edward I* (New York and London, 1997).

Quinnell, H. and Blockley, M. with Berridge, P. *Excavations at Rhuddlan, Clwyd, 1969–73* (York, 1994).

Soulsby, I. *The Towns of Medieval Wales*, (Chichester, 1983).

Taylor, A.J. 'Harlech Castle: The Dating of the Outer Enclosure', *Journal of the Merioneth Historical Society*, 1 (1949–51), 202–3.

Taylor, A.J. 'Master James of St. George', *English Historical Review*, LXV (1950), 433-457.

Taylor, A.J. 'The Date of Caernarfon Castle', *Antiquity*, 26 (1952), 25–34.

Taylor, A.J. 'Castle-Building in Thirteenth-Century Wales and Savoy', *Proceedings of the British Academy*, 63 (1977), 265–92.

Taylor, A.J. *Four Great Castles: Caernarfon, Conwy, Harlech, Beaumaris* (Newtown, 1983).

Taylor, A.J. *Studies in Castles and Castle-Building* (Hambledon Continuum, London, 1985)

Taylor, Arnold *The Welsh Castles of Edward I* (London, 1986). Appeared previously as *The History of the King's Works* in Colvin cited above.

Taylor, A.J. *Rhuddlan Castle* (Cardiff, 1987).

Thompson, M.W. *The Rise of the Castle* (Cambridge University Press,1991).

Thompson, M.W. *The Decline of the Castle* (Cambridge University Press, 1988).

Turnbull, D. 'Some Problems about the Origin of Criccieth Castle', *Fort*, 7 (1979), 52–68.

Glossary

Apse A rounded end.

Ashlar Smooth, flat masonry blocks.

Bailey A courtyard.

Ballista A projectile engine resembling a giant crossbow, utilizing the tension of a bow or the torsion of two arms thrust through skeins of cord. Usually for shooting large arrows or bolts.

Bar hole A hole in a wall into which a drawbar slides.

Barbican An outwork that protects a gate.

Barrel vault A cylindrical plain stone vault.

Batter The base of a wall thickened with a sloping front.

Belfry A wooden tower, often mobile, used either to overlook a wall or to transfer troops on to it.

Berm The space between a wall and ditch.

Brattice Wooden hoarding built out from a battlement to command the base of a wall.

Buttress Stone support built against a wall to reinforce it.

Corbel A supporting stone bracket.

Countermine A tunnel dug from a castle aimed at breaking into an enemy mineshaft.

Counterscarp The outer slope of a ditch.

Crenel The open section of a battlement.

Crenellation Battlement.

Cross-vault A vault in which two barrel vaults intersect.

Curtain A length of wall surrounding a castle or town.

Daub A filling used to cover wattle walling, made from mud or clay sometimes mixed with dung and straw.

Donjon A great tower or keep, but it can also refer to an upper bailey or lord's private area.

Drawbar A wooden beam for securing the inside of a door, which runs back into a hole in the wall to allow the door to open.

Échaugette A look-out post or turret built on the battlements of a wall section.

Embrasure An internal opening in a wall, sometimes for the use of archers.

Enceinte The area enclosed by the castle walls.

Great tower See donjon.

Groined vault A cross-vault whose edges are sharply defined.

Hoarding See **brattice**.

Jamb The side of an opening through a wall.

Joggled Keyed together by overlapping joints.

Keep A word used in England from the 16th century to describe a donjon.

Loop A narrow opening in a wall that splays out internally, designed either to admit light or for shooting through.

Machicolation Battlement brought forward on corbels to allow soldiers to command the base of a wall.

Mangonel Variously used to describe a torsion catapult utilizing a skein of cord as a spring, or a trebuchet, often the type utilizing manpower.

Merlon The solid section of a battlement.

Mine A tunnel dug under a wall to weaken the foundations and bring it down.

Moat A ditch, either wet or dry.

Motte An earth mound.

Mural chamber A vaulted chamber formed in the thickness of a wall.

Mural passage A vaulted passage formed in the thickness of a wall.

Mural tower A tower set along a curtain wall.

Murder hole A hole in a passage vault or ceiling through which offensive material could be dropped on attackers, or water to douse fires.

Parados A low, inner wall of a wall-walk.

Parapet The outer wall of a wall-walk.

Petrary A stone-throwing catapult.

Pilaster A shallow pier built against a wall to buttress it.

Portcullis A lattice made from wood clad in iron, or occasionally in iron alone, dropped to block a gate.

Postern A small rear door.

Putlog A hole in a wall designed to take the beams that support scaffolding.

Rampart An earthen bank.

Revetment The side of a ditch, bank or motte faced with wood, stone or brick.

Ring-work A circular or oval earthwork with bank and ditch.

Scarp The side of a ditch.

Spur A solid, pointed stone reinforcement at the base of a tower; also, a finger of high ground.

Trebuchet A catapult whose throwing arm utilizes the principle of counterbalance.

Truss A timber frame designed to support a roof.

Turning bridge A bridge like a see-saw, the rear half falling into a pit as the front section is raised.

Turret A small tower.

Vault A curved ceiling of stone.

Vice A spiral stair.

Wall-walk A passage along the top of a wall.

Ward See **bailey**.

Wattle Stakes interwoven with branches, used for walling.

Index